"Look up and stay in touch"

Slater Bradley & Ed Lachman

Aspen Art Press | Aspen Art Museum

Contents

Don't let me disappear

Slater Bradley might just be the unintended king of serendipity. The number of times that I have thought about him and then, within moments, had my mobile phone ring, with his voice on the other end of the line, is too many to chalk up to coincidence. I finally stopped saying, "I was just thinking about you," to which he had always answered, "Of course."

We met by chance when a car I was in pulled over to the side of the road at night in Miami in 2002; he joined us in the back seat. I was with curators Amada Cruz, who was organizing a show with Slater at the time, Dominic Molon, and Rochelle Steiner. It was the year of the first Art Basel Miami Beach. Curiosity ran high, as did hope. Later that night I asked Slater what he thought people liked about his work. I have subsequently been able to answer that question for myself. I have been privileged to organize a solo exhibition of his work at the Berkeley Art Museum, where we produced a film in which Ben Brock, Slater's long-time doppelganger and collaborator, drummed the beat of Led Zeppelin's "When the Levee Breaks" just weeks before the tragedy of Hurricane Katrina affected New Orleans. While at Berkeley Slater sent me a postcard with a painting by Pieter Brueghel on the front and a phrase by the literary protagonist Holden Caulfield on the back: "Please don't let me disappear." Although the text was appropriated, like many of the personas that appear in his videos, its directness was simultaneously pointed and haunting and filled me with a sense of responsibility for the artist and the person.

A few years later, at my urging Slater finished *Protector of the Kennel III* (2006), a video work for a 2006 show I curated for the Aspen Art Museum entitled *Belief and Doubt*. The show was dedicated to one of my closest friends, someone who had died recently and tragically. In retrospect, completing *Protector of the Kennel III* saved all of us. How? The action gave purpose to the artist and additional meaning to my thoughts. In the work, Bradley's doppelganger walks through Central Park in New York performing his day job, walking dogs. As Slater filmed, kids in the park started to follow Ben and the dogs serendipitously. He became a symbol of attraction and guidance—a messenger of some sort who metaphorically carried the knowledge that one can often neither control to whom they are attracted, nor for what or whom they become responsible. Both inside that work and outside it (that is, in life/reality watching it unfold), subject and object became conflated. Boundaries collapsed.

This past December I ran into Slater in Miami again. He had stayed on for an extra day, unsure what propelled him to not leave. We talked about his latest project, in which the doppelganger dies. In a cyclical relationship that has covered birth, death, and resurgence, I probably don't need to explain that showing the project felt fated.

Look Up and Stay in Touch is a collaboration with the director and Academy Award–nominated cinematographer Ed Lachman, the director of photography for the film *Dark Blood*, an unreleased 1993 film starring River Phoenix that was in production during the time of Phoenix's death. In *Dark Blood*, Phoenix plays a young, disturbed, half-Navajo widower who lives in seclusion near a nuclear testing site in the Nevada desert, waiting for the apocalypse and making kachina dolls that he believes have magic powers. The film progresses to a dramatic ending in which the young man dies, but because of Phoenix's own untimely death, the final scenes were never filmed. *Shadow* (2010) is based on Lachman's memories of working on the original film some seventeen years prior. It is conceived as a prologue that imagines the widower's life just before meeting the stranded couple. The work mixes references to the original film with references to the film's production—*Shadow* was filmed in the same location, near the Capitol Reef in Utah, and utilizes sets and artifacts from *Dark Blood*, like the bar Phoenix frequented during production and snapshots of Phoenix and Lachman working on the film that the artists happened upon inside the bar. This mixing of fiction and reality, restaging and reimagining, becomes a simultaneous portrait of Phoenix, Bradley, and Lachman, all channeled through the doppelganger.

Along with *Shadow* the project includes *Dead Ringer* (2011), a three-channel video installation that simultaneously presents three different takes of the same shot. The work progresses in the order the shots were made, and not according to the linear narrative of the film, and minor variations in the movement and speech between each version create a beautifully unsettling rhythm. The serendipity of the takes working together hints at the fortuitous moments that run throughout all of Bradley's works.

Just as Slater is driven to prevent Ian Curtis, Kurt Cobain, Michael Jackson, John Bonham, and now River Phoenix from disappearing, I too am committed to the saving of Slater Bradley: Slater Bradley who for the last eight years has placed his doppelganger in front of the camera, a stand-in for himself. I have written previously that the doppelganger has enacted a vast array of activities that Slater himself may have wished to perform. My commitment is to the real Slater Bradley. The one who stepped in front of the camera for the first time in *Dead Ringer*, only to kill the doppelganger once and for all and reclaim his self, the ultimate end ringing of serendipity. Slater explained how it actually happened on set. I replied, "Of course."

Heidi Zuckerman Jacobson
Chief Executive Officer and Director, Chief Curator

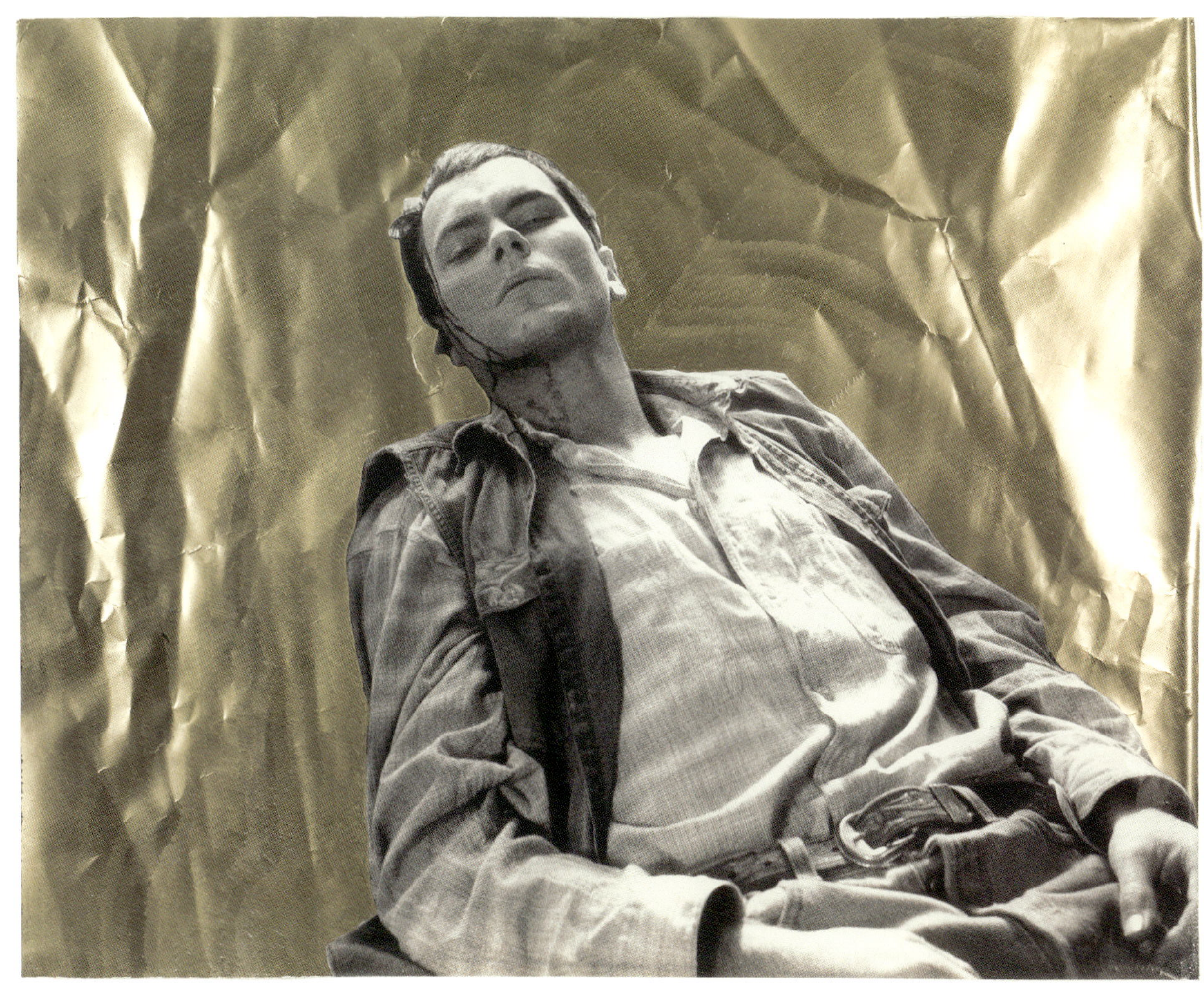

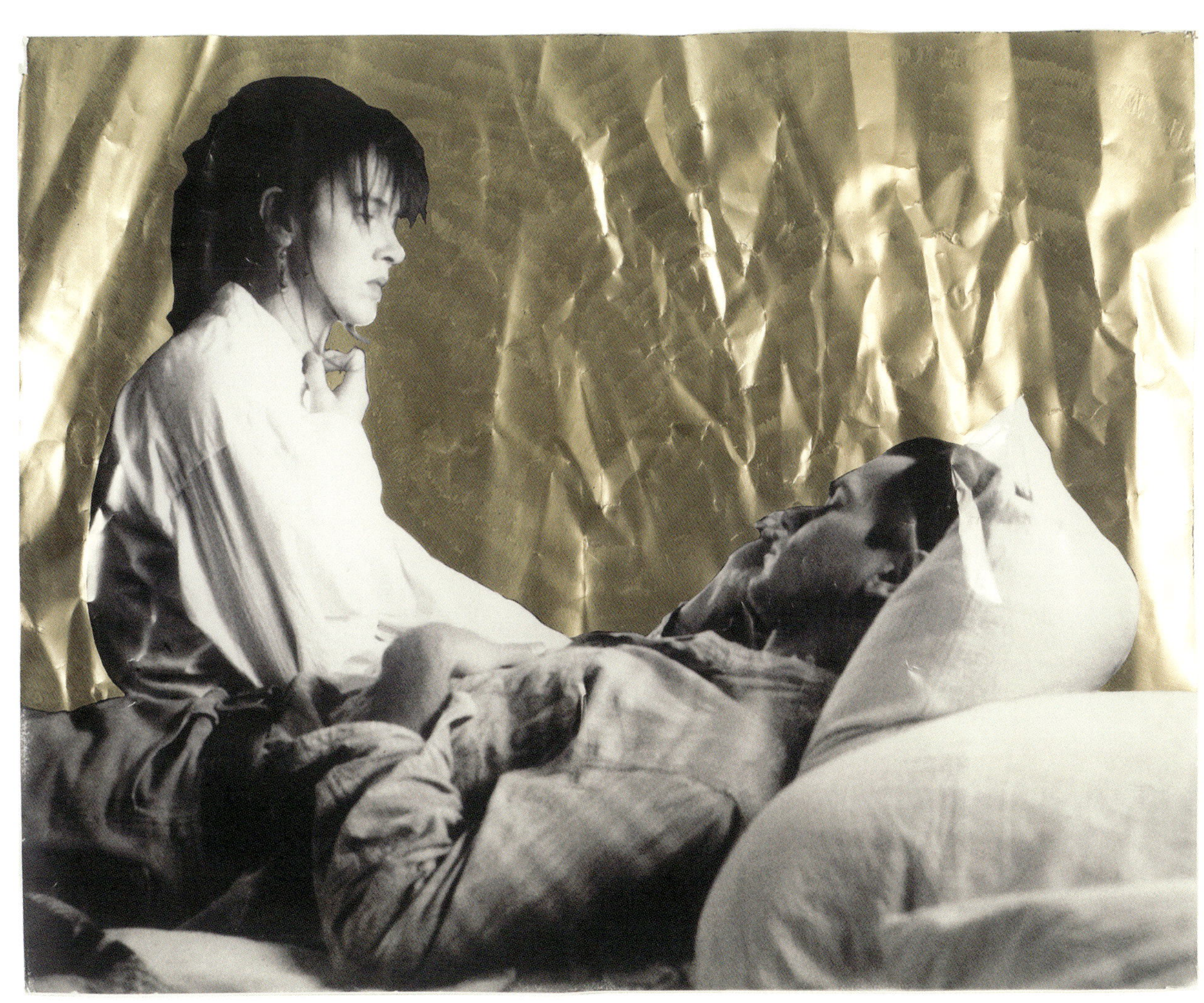

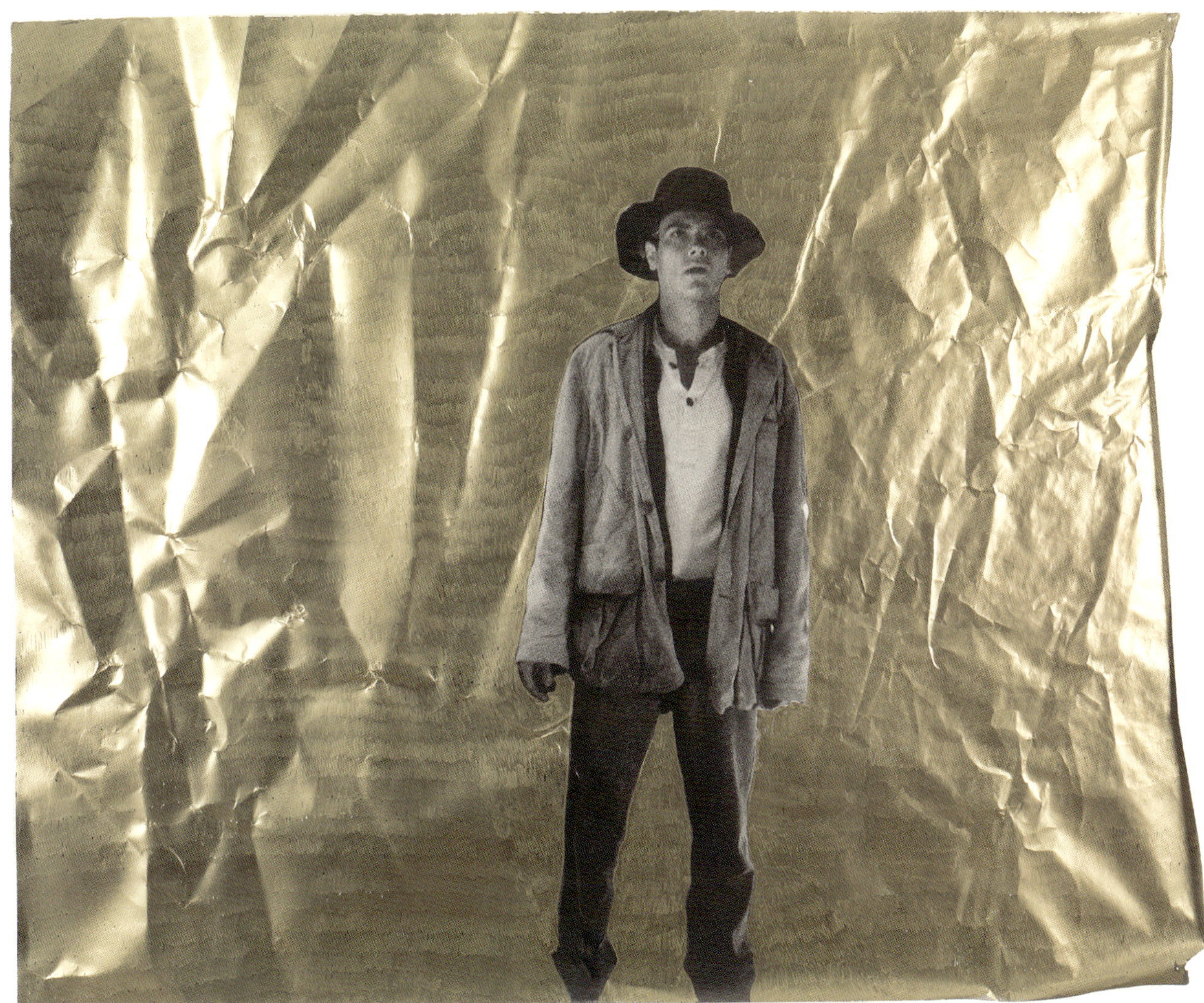

Chrissie Iles

The Shadow of the Gaze
Slater Bradley and the Uncanny

In the early 1920s, towards the end of his life, Claude Monet stood on the Japanese bridge over the ornamental water lily pond in his garden at Giverny and took a photograph of his shadow. His head, wearing a hat, can be seen reflected in the surface of the water, barely visible at the periphery of the black-and-white photograph's bottom edge. The ghostly presence of the artist in Monet's enigmatic self-portrait anticipates Slater Bradley's doppelganger project eighty years later, in which the double operates as a mechanism through which to interrogate the transience and permeability of identity.

Monet's self-portrait appeared at the same moment, in the early 1920s, that Duchamp was constructing, in works such as *L.H.O.O.Q.* (1919) and *Monte Carlo Bond* (1924) and in Man Ray's portrait of Duchamp as Rrose Sélavy (1921), an encounter with the self as readymade. As David Joselit argues, this encounter, at a moment when capitalism was beginning to construct the first technologically driven consumer culture, involved a confrontation with the shadow self in the process of commodification, as masquerade.[1] Within this context, it is perhaps not far-fetched to suggest that Manet's hat could be read not as the standard dress of an early-twentieth-century man outside in the open air, but as a quiet theatrical gesture by a master from an older generation at the end of his life, registering the dramatic changes that the new photographic technology was beginning to effect in the perceiving self, and using that technology

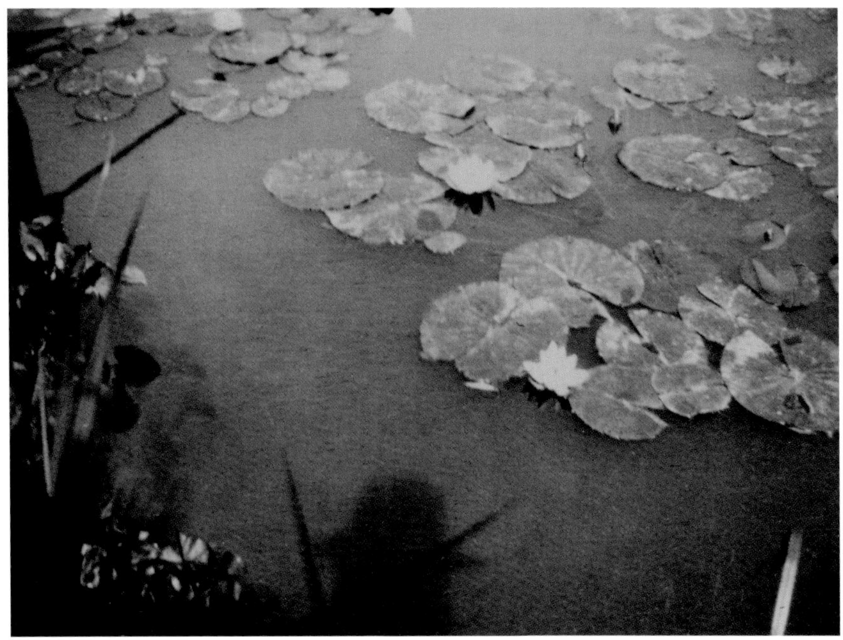

to create a shadowy self–portrait bordering on the cinematic that evokes Victor Stoichita's observation that for the Greeks, "the silhouette [was] the immaterial double of the one who was leaving."[2]

The confrontation of the shadow self through masquerade described by Joselit, and its implications for mortality, find their echo in Bradley's doppelganger project, the first video of which was created in 2001, at a similar moment of dramatic technological, social, and cultural transformation. Like Duchamp's project, Bradley's project reveals identity to be a construct by filtering it through different personae. But Bradley's and Duchamp's projects differ in several important ways that indicate the specific cultural anxiety of the historical moments within which they occur. Whilst Duchamp's fracturing of the self takes place within the framework of a sexually ambiguous doubling (Duchamp becomes the feminine Rrose Sélavy; a mass-produced photographic reproduction of Leonardo's *Mona Lisa* is made masculine by the application to her face of a moustache and beard), Bradley's fractured self adopts an historical, literary manifestation of the doubled self, the doppelganger, whose identity, like Bradley's shadow selves, is always male.

Furthermore, Duchamp's alter egos—R. Mutt, Belle Helaine, Marchand Du Sel, Archy Pen Co., Marsélavy, the wanted criminal Hook, Lyon and Cinquer, Sarah Bernhardt, a monkish ascetic and a shaving-cream smothered satyr—are all imaginary forms of himself, acted out by him and constructed, conceptually and photographically, with Man Ray, whilst in Bradley's project the artist's personae are doppelgangers of real people— Kurt Cobain, Ian Curtis, Michael Jackson, and River Phoenix—all iconic figures from contemporary popular music and cinema, tragically deceased, and acted out by the young actor and model Ben Brock, who superficially resembles Bradley and takes on the role of his—and the icons'—alter ego. Bradley thus uses the blank screen that Brock's role as an actor and model represents as a symbolic projective surface. Whilst Duchamp uses invented versions of himself as a form of reproduction, to undermine the fixity of identity and interpretation, Bradley's doppelgangers are invented versions of deceased figures from popular culture, invested with the artist's wish to identify with their symbolic power. If Duchamp's project is a conceptual interrogation of the self through a mirroring process, Bradley's, using the shadow, rather than the mirror, as the self's representational model, demonstrates the shadow's ancient, primary purpose: to make the absent present and to immortalize that presence. Bradley's shadow selves are thus predicated not on distance, like Duchamp's, but on desire.

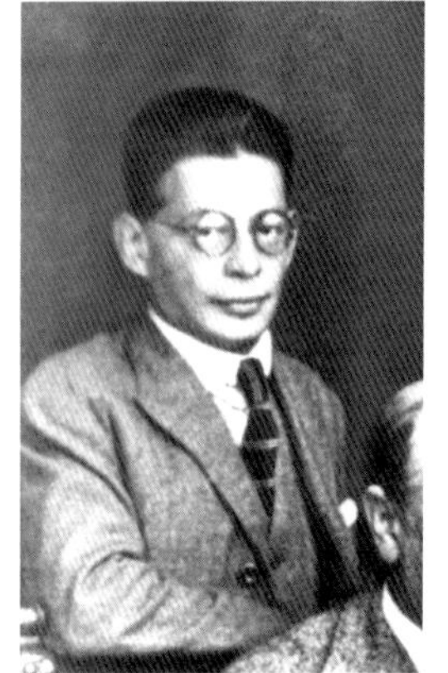

Otto Rank

This desire is, arguably, a condition of the doppelganger itself, one of the oldest symbolic figures in the Western world, whose aim, as the Austrian psychoanalyst Otto Rank points out, is not only to shadow the person, but to take them over completely: "Then I saw you, and wanted to become your You—but that won't work, for I cannot go back; but you can go on ahead, one of these days you will become my Self."[3] Bradley internalizes this vampiric instinct by duplicating the doppelganger's role; whilst Brock operates as Bradley's doppelganger, his personification of icons from popular culture who no longer exist ultimately renders Bradley *their* doppelganger. In this triangle of shadows, it is not Brock who takes over Bradley, but Bradley who takes over, symbolically, the icons that he duplicates, in a performative masquerade of self-portraiture.

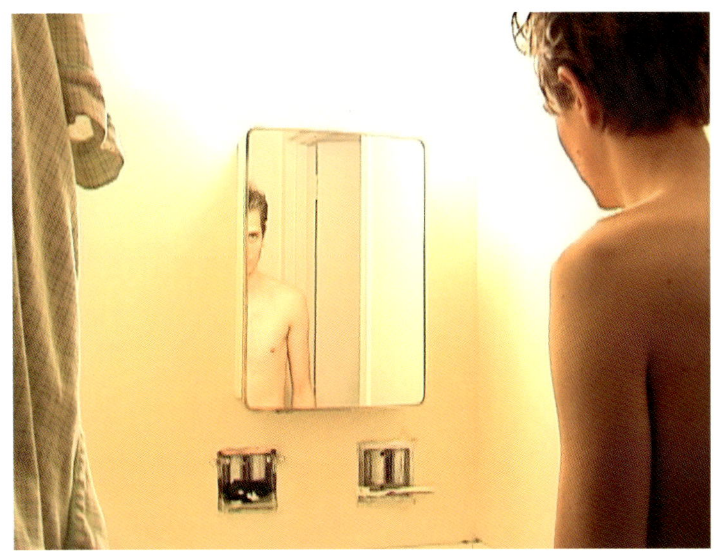

Slater Bradley, *Trompe Le Monde*, 2001.

This performative core of Bradley's project is underscored by Andrew Webber's description of the doppelganger as one who "echoes, reiterates, distorts, parodies, dictates, impedes and dumbfounds the subjective faculty of free speech… The doppelganger is a performer of identity. Indeed, it could be said to represent the performative character of the subject. Selfhood as a metaphysical given is abandoned… to a process of enactments of identity always mediated by the other self. The performances of the doppelganger are so many rehearsals of the double role on various reconstructions of the Lacanian mirror stage."[4]

The double meaning of "stage" in Webber's text is deliberate and provides a useful tool with which to discuss the performative structure of Bradley's doppelganger project and how it negotiates the boundary between reality and fiction. Brock's performances in Bradley's video installations, photographs, and paintings all take place on a literal or figurative stage, on which real and fictive situations are played out by a person who is always a double playing the role of someone else.

In *Trompe Le Monde* (2001), Bradley's first doppelganger video work, Brock acts out Bradley's daily routine in Bradley's apartment, then walks into the elevator, goes downstairs, and disappears down the street. Brock's final action (echoed in *Ghost* [2001], in which Brock, playing the double

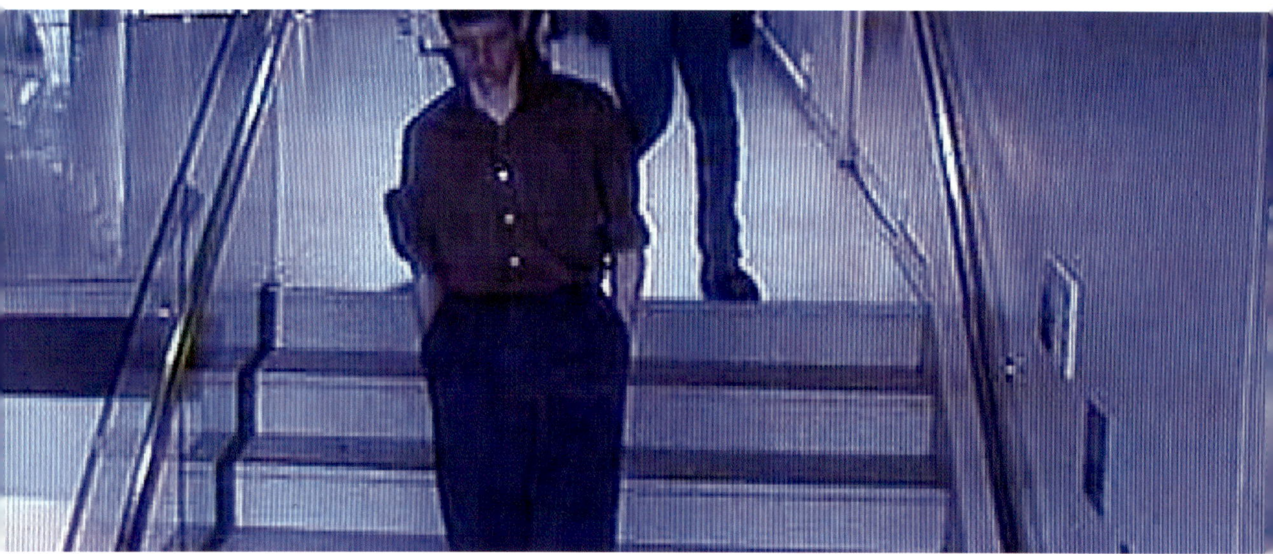

Slater Bradley, *Ghost*, 2001.

of Ian Curtis and filmed by a security camera, walks into a museum then leaves) evokes a moment in the classic doppelganger film *The Student of Prague* (1913) in which the student "is numbed with astonishment when he sees his alter-ego detach itself from the mirror and follow the old man through the door and out upon the street."[5] The elusive presence of Brock's body, seen in fragments through the camera's framing and by its multiple reflections in the elevator mirrors, is heightened by Bradley's manipulation of the video image. Its degraded black-and-white surface evokes the degraded texture of surveillance camera footage, dislocating the imagery from its everyday context and lending it a phantasmagoric cast.

The reduction in contrast between foreground and background in this depiction of Brock's ghostly presence evokes Plato's definition of the visible world according to "degrees of clarity and obscurity," within which the shadow, unlike the mirror or other reflective surfaces, is dark, undifferentiated, and nocturnal.[6] Plato's observation accrues a psychological and technological metaphor in Webber's observation that in the double, "the real is duplicated as phantasm in such a way as to defy distinction," describing this ambiguity of distinction in the doppelganger, or "spook," as having "something of the effect of a photographic negative."[7]

The photograph is, arguably, a form of a shadow, in the sense that it is inextricably linked to its subject, and acts as a trace of that subject's presence. In Bradley's doppelganger project, the images of the three iconic figures of Curtis, Cobain, and Jackson, whether rendered in video, photography, or painting, are all photographically generated, and their surfaces often altered, and the background stripped away. This abstracting of the central figure evokes medieval Byzantine painting, in which the image, a silhouette depicted against a background of gold, was a soul, or spirit, made visible, and not of this world. The image had no shadow precisely because *it* was a shadow—a doppelganger of an invisible spiritual being.

The concept of the shadow self as a manifestation of the soul has existed since the early writings of Plato; but in 1925, Otto Rank argued that the public had become increasingly drawn to the theme of the double, or shadow likeness, at moments of war, or great social and political upheaval. The unsettling impact of these moments of collective trauma triggered an inquiry into the integrity of the self and the contradictions contained within it. Bradley became preoccupied with the doppelganger theme after immersing himself in nineteenth-century Russian and European literature, in which the doppelganger consistently appeared, and at a moment of collective uncertainty at the end of the millennium, when the impact of the technological revolution signaled by the advent of the Internet was transforming the social, political, and cultural landscape.

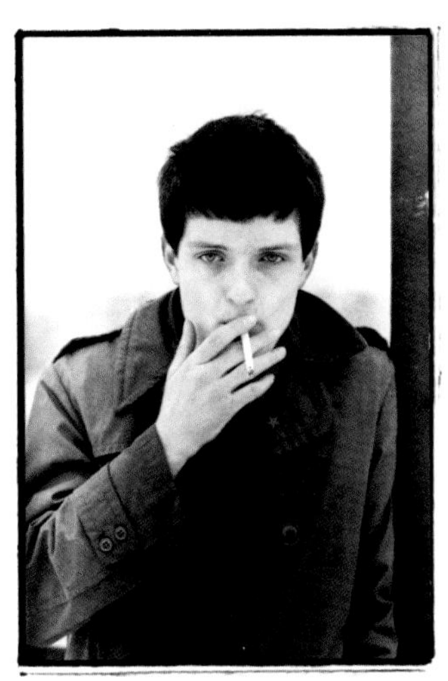

Kevin Cummins, *Ian Curtis,* 1979.

The Doppelganger Trilogy, a group of three video installations, began in 2001, shortly after one of the greatest moments of collective trauma in American history, September 11, had occurred. Brock appears in each one, playing the roles of Curtis, Cobain, and Jackson performing imagined concerts. In *Factory Archives* (2001–2), Brock aka Ian Curtis, the lead singer of the legendary 1980s Manchester band Joy Division, is seen through the grainy haze of an apparently old, low-resolution, amateur videotape of the kind that an enterprising fan would have made at a Joy Division concert before the days of MTV, smart phones, and YouTube.

Bradley's appropriation of an out-of-date technology, apparently recording the performance of one of the most iconic tragic musical figures of the 1980s, uses anachronism to underscore the rendering of his subject as unreal. In a further twist, the videotape is a reworking of a tape made independently by Brock in 2000, of himself performing as Ian Curtis, to submit as an audition for the film *Transmission,* on the life and death of Ian Curtis, the script for which was written by Bradley's friend Michael Stock. Bradley manipulates the video image until Brock is almost invisible, weaving past moments in the history of Curtis's life and work into a ghostly projection in which Brock operates both as Bradley's doppelganger and as his own double, expressing his own, as well as Bradley's, desire to act the role of Curtis, within three different time frames—the fictional historical moment, the actual moment of the later audition, and the actual moment that the piece was made—collapsed into the two parallel narrative structures of art and cinema.

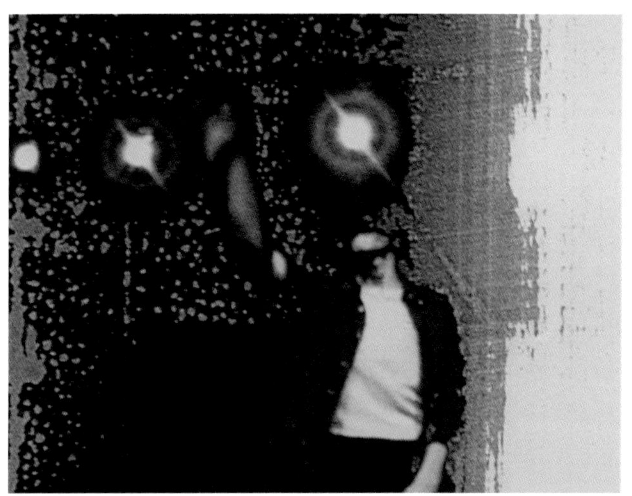

Slater Bradley, *Recorded Yesterday,* 2004.

In the third video of the trilogy, *Recorded Yesterday* (2004), Brock plays Michael Jackson, filmed by Bradley in black and white with a Super 8 camera as he executes Jackson's dance steps on the empty stage of a theater in New York. The glamorous showmanship of the star, in his 1980s heyday, is rendered melancholic and almost invisible, except for a clear trace of Jackson's brilliance left deliberately evident in Brock's meticulous study of his host's form.

These twists and turns of Bradley's complex doubling reflect the classic doppelganger form. As Webber explains, in Romantic literature, the doppelganger "embodies a dislocation in time, always coming after its proper event. Like all ghosts, it is at once an historical figure, representing past times, and a profoundly anti-historical phenomenon, stepping out of time…. [it] returns, inter-textually, from one text to the other. Its performances repeat both its host subject and its own previous appearances, so it plays a constitutive role in the structuring of its texts, by doubling them back upon themselves. This function of return will be read as 'unheimlich'—the uncanny—in the Freudian sense."[8]

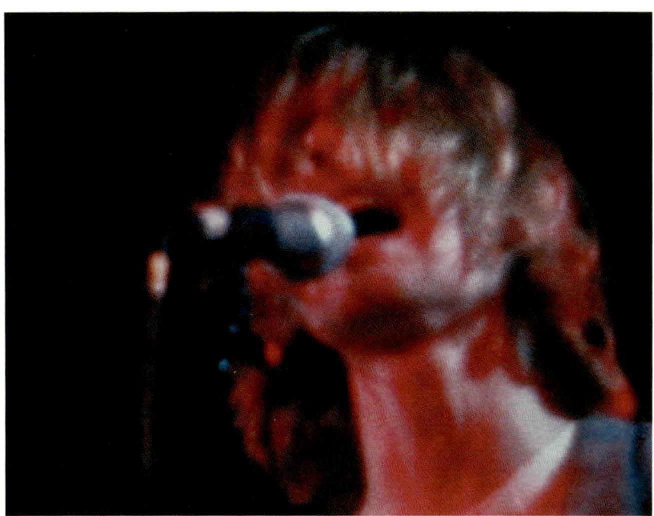

Slater Bradley, *Phantom Release,* 2003.

Bradley's doppelganger works epitomize this mechanism; the multiple doublings, and sometimes triplings, that occur operate as both a harbinger of death, a confirmation that it has already occurred, and the possibility that, through the shadow, it might be defeated. This paradox, built into Bradley and Brock's relationship from the beginning, evokes Richard Meyer's observation in 1916 of German Romantic author E. T. A. Hoffmann's literary doppelgangers: "[they are] unsure of their identity, are sometimes inhabitants of this earth, and sometimes belong to some unearthly region."[9]

This uncertain state of being becomes evident once again in *Phantom Release* (2003), the second video in the *Doppelganger Trilogy*. Kurt Cobain, played by Brock, is seen playing guitar with his band, Nirvana, in an exact replica of the band's clothes and instruments. The degraded, saturated Super 8 Kodachrome video image of Brock's nameless, placeless performance suggests the quality of an amateur recording by an unknown fan, positioning the action as a disembodied, unidentifiable masquerade.

The complex duplication of Bradley's doppelgangers within this indefinable sense of place demonstrates what Marvin Carlson terms "ghosting," a technique in which an audience experiences "the identical thing they have encountered before, although now in a somewhat different context. Thus a recognition not of similarity… but of identity becomes part of the reception process." Ghosting is quite common in theater, Carlson explains, giving an example he experienced in which "we witnessed Blumenfeld ghosted by Nathan Lane ghosted by Sid Caesar ghosted by Marlon Brando playing Brutus ghosted by his interpretation of Stanley Kowalski."[10]

Carlson's description of the ghosting process as a theatrical mechanism confirms Bradley's doppelgangers as essentially performative subjects, which, as Webber argues, are "more or less pathologically divided between reality and fantasy." The doppelganger is fictional, but it cannot be written off as phantasm; "it insists on its place in the real… the subjective spook at once threatens and underpins the objective claims of realism."[11]

This uncertain boundary between reality and fantasy, by which all Bradley's doppelganger performances are defined, signifies a crisis in selfhood that finds its historical precedent in the nineteenth century's emergent mediums of photography and cinema, and in particular their capacity to produce a double image through the use of "replicating instruments" such as lenses, masks, and the split screen. "In a diary note," Dietrich Scheunemann observes, E. T. A. Hoffmann "clearly establishes the connection between the use of replicating instruments and the [doppelganger's] primary function to question a unified concept of identity: 'I think of myself through a replicating glass.'"[12]

For Bradley, this location of the doppelganger within the cinematic created a logical context for his final doppelganger work: a collaboration with the acclaimed cinematographer Ed Lachman, with whom he created two video installations and a group of photographic works based on the young Hollywood actor River Phoenix. One of the basic tenets of cinema, as

Christian Metz has observed, is the depiction of space as a kind of mirror in which the spectator, in the space of the real world, cannot see themselves. In this paradoxical situation, with what, then, does the viewer identify? With the person behind the camera, Metz answers. The cinematographer thus becomes the spectator's shadow; a ghostly presence whose symbolic duplication of the viewer produces a filmic condition of the uncanny.

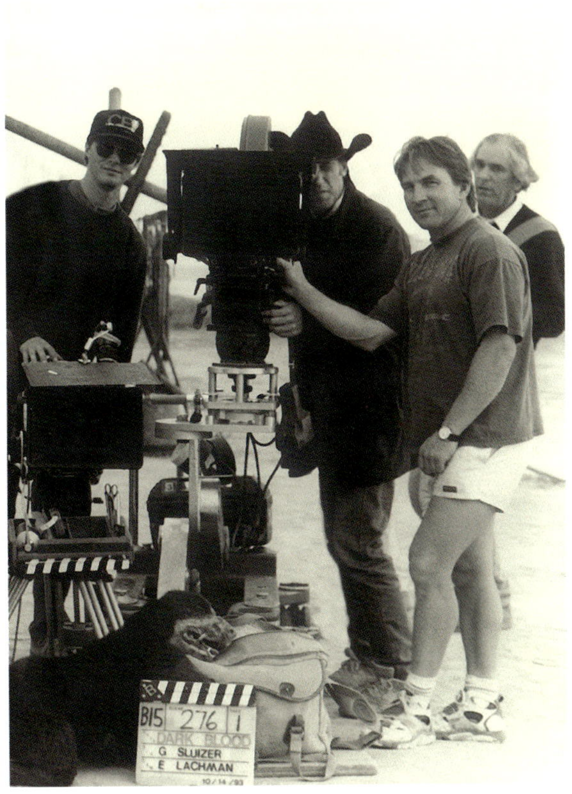

Ed Lachman (center) and crew on the set of *Dark Blood* (George Sluizer, 1993).

It is this condition of the uncanny, and its implications for identity, that Bradley and Lachman articulate in *Shadow* (2010). The innate projective cast of the shadow, in both literal and figurative terms, arguably renders it inherently cinematic, a state underlined by its fleeting temporality. Reliant for its existence on a precise moment that renders it continually in the process of disappearing, the shadow, like film, always operates in the space between being and becoming. The meaning of *Shadow* is predicated on the perceptual and psychological implications of this liminal state. *Shadow* is a film about its shadow; it is also the shadow of a film that exists, but remains invisible, inaccessible, and unfinished.

In 1993, Lachman spent several weeks in the desert in Utah shooting *Dark Blood,* a Hollywood film starring River Phoenix. Phoenix plays a disturbed young half-Navajo widower who lives like a hermit on a nuclear testing site in the Nevada desert, waiting for the apocalypse, and mourning the death of his wife, who was killed by radiation from the test site. A married couple traveling across the desert become stranded in their car and are rescued by the boy, who falls in love with the woman. The film progresses to a dramatic ending in which the boy is shot dead by the man and becomes engulfed in flames as Navajo Indians burn down the shack to which he has been taken. Towards the end of the shooting, River Phoenix died of a drug overdose in Los Angeles, leaving the film unfinished.

Seventeen years later, *Shadow* constructs a prologue based on Lachman's memory of shooting the original film that imagines the widower immediately before he meets the couple, folding into the story a number of references to what takes place in the future in the original film. Elements of the original film—the couple, the car breaking down, the attraction of the widower to the woman—do not appear in Bradley and Lachman's film, and parts of their narrative—a little girl, a deserted house, a bar—do not appear in the original. Other elements appear in both films, creating a complex structure in which the two narratives are woven together by threads of fact and fiction, whose boundaries are never made clear.

This deliberate obfuscation of the line between reality and fiction is the lens through which Bradley and Lachman's enquiry into the shadow self is filtered. Bradley's interest in the ill-fated film that Lachman had shot in 1993 was partly predicated on the portent of death that Phoenix's untimely end evoked and its symbolic implications for both the unfinished film and for Bradley's doppelganger project. The collaboration between artist and cinematographer produced a unique fusion of art and cinema, in which Bradley's engagement with the doppelganger took on a narrative cinematic complexity that, in turn, gave voice to the more conceptual aspects of Lachman's cinematographic thinking. As Lachman wrote in his notebook during the making of *Shadow*, "One creates an illusion in reality, but what is reality but an illusion? So I re-visited the illusion to find what's left of the reality."[13]

Lachman's note pinpoints the core of the doppelganger's meaning. *Shadow*'s structure of repeated doubling is defined through its relationship to *Dark Blood* both as a film and as the recovered event of an abandoned film shoot. The literary model of the doppelganger's continual return is echoed in *Shadow* in numerous ways. Lachman, whose participation in *Dark Blood* occurred as a cinematographer, reappears in *Shadow* as a coauthor, this time shooting not River Phoenix but his invented doppelganger Brock, who is, in turn, simultaneously the doppelganger of Bradley, thus also implicating Bradley as the doppelganger of Phoenix. Lachman's memory of shooting the original film becomes another kind of duplication, creating, as is so often the case in Bradley's work, not a doubling but a tripling, in this case comprised of *Dark Blood*, Lachman's memory of shooting that film, and the new film, *Shadow*, that emerged from both.

The doubles in *Shadow*, the most complex of Bradley's doppelganger works, occur as figurative, as well as literal, duplications. Lachman and Bradley chose the same desert location for *Shadow* in which Phoenix had originally acted the same character. As Lachman observed, "creating a shadow landscape created some way for me to enter the original landscape and find a new narrative."[14] Numerous other ghostings of the original film are folded into Lachman and Bradley's intertextual drama. The centerfold pinup from *Playboy*, which the boy, played by Brock, burns in a fire in the night in the desert at the end of *Shadow*, echoes the erotic presence of the woman in *Dark Blood* with whom the boy falls in unrequited love. Her image disappears in the flames just like the dead boy disappeared in the flames when the Navajo Indians set fire to his hut at the end of *Dark Blood*. In *Shadow* Bradley and Lachman reverse the characters' roles, giving the boy his revenge as he watches her disappear into the flames.

Another layer of doubling takes place when Lachman comes out from behind the camera by appearing in *Shadow* in a photograph of himself and Phoenix taken on the set of *Dark Blood* during a break in filming, which Lachman and Bradley found by chance on the location of the original film. In *Shadow* Brock finds the photograph at the bar, tucked inside another issue of *Playboy*, which the boy collects—a detail that appears in the original script. When Brock sees the photograph, he is confronted with the original actor whom he is portraying, photographed as himself rather than in character, in a dramatic breaking of the fourth wall that momentarily exposes the reality of the doppelganger's doubling to the audience.

Just as the theatrical experience described by Carlson depends on the recognition of each actor's ghosting of the next, *Shadow*'s meaning depends on the viewer's recognition of its difference from *Dark Blood*. Lachman and Bradley intensify the conceptual significance of this difference in a second, three-screen video installation titled *Dead Ringer* (2011), the final work in Bradley's doppelganger project. Tripling appears repeatedly in Bradley's work, as a device through which, as Paul Fleming observes, the doppelganger's transfiguration can be made evident.[15] It appears here in the form of three apparently identical video projections that are revealed, on close inspection, to be three different takes of a climactic moment of the

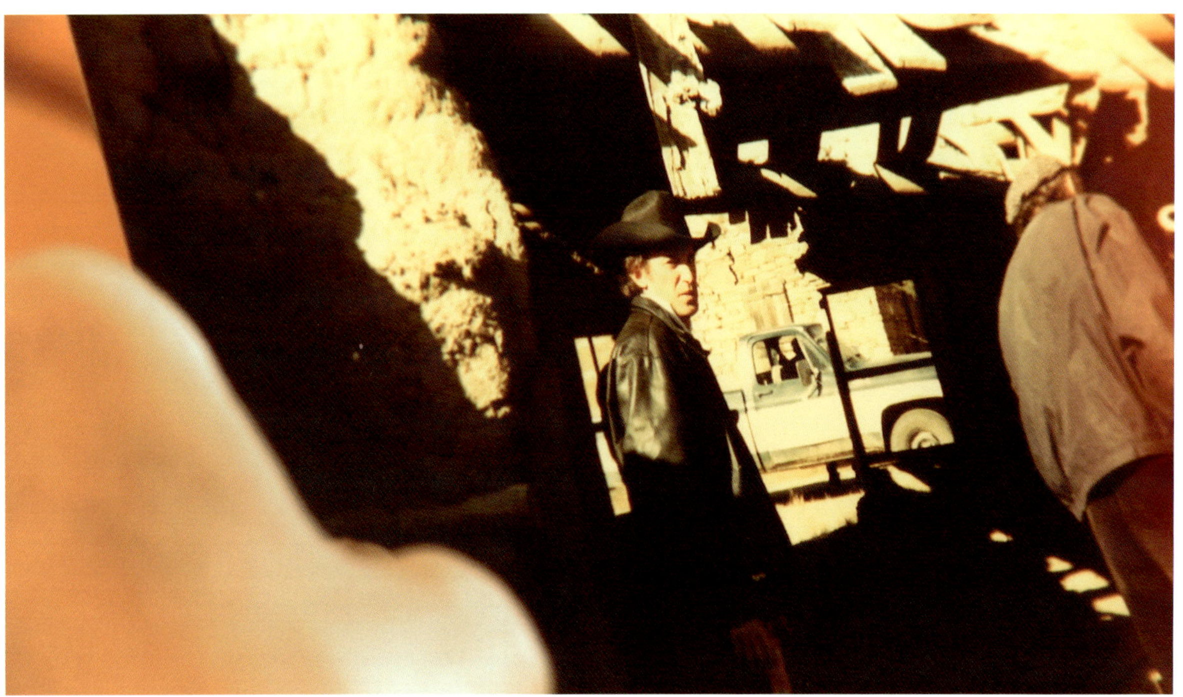

Slater Bradley and Ed Lachman, *Shadow*, 2010.

final scene of *Dark Blood*. Each take, slightly different from the other, ghosts the last, creating, in true doppelganger form, a circular repetition of its own previous appearance.

In the shot, framed against the stark beauty of the Utah desert, Brock plays River Phoenix playing the boy immediately after he witnesses the husband

killing his dog after a struggle between the two men in which the husband
fatally wounds the boy with an axe. Brock confronts the husband, played
by Bradley who, like Lachman, appears for the first time and, by his actions
and presence, both predicts and effects the death of his doppelganger, who,
in the script for *Dark Blood,* dies shortly afterwards. Bradley and Lachman's
triptych illustrates Webber's argument that the doppelganger is "above all
a figure of visual compulsion… The self-seeing subject beholds its other
self as another, as visual object, or alternatively, is beheld as object by its
other self."[16]

The impending death predicted by Bradley's character in *Dead Ringer* and
scripted in *Dark Blood* was never, owing to Phoenix's own death, finally
completed. The only trace of the unfinished final death scene exists in a
group of black-and-white Polaroid photographs taken by Lachman on
the set, in order to check the light. In a group of painterly photographic
works, Lachman and Bradley transform these images, enlarging them into
otherworldly compositions in which Phoenix floats suspended against
a gold background, devoid of any shading. In one group, a Polaroid of
Phoenix, playing the boy on his deathbed, is collaged against a solid gold
background, and the paper has been crumpled, in a metaphorical gesture
that suggests the discarded usefulness effected by the actor's untimely death.
In another, he appears surrounded by a halo of gold-leaf dust. As Stoichita
observes, in ancient Egypt, it was believed that two kinds of shadows
existed: a dark shadow that confirmed the living presence of a person
by its delineation of their physical body; and after death, a clear shadow,
or "ka," which took over the function of the double. Like the degraded
surfaces of the doppelganger videos, the lack of dark shadows in Bradley
and Lachman's painterly photographic images evoke this second shadow,
indicating Phoenix's status as an immaterial being, whose "diaphanous
body… allows the rays of the sun to pass through," radiating a symbolic
cultural power.[17]

These haunting images of Phoenix, suspended in ethereal immateriality,
recall the delicate surface of the shadow self-portrait by Monet that began
this text. As Stoichita argues, in choosing to photograph his shadow
reflected in the same water that he depicted in his paintings, "Monet's own

shadow is etched on the surface of the representation like a figurative and paradoxical feature of a dual symbol of presence/transience."[18] Bradley's doppelganger project creates a similar fusion of the artist with his subject, symbolically etching himself onto the surface of his representation in a continuous performative rehearsal of his own death.

1   David Joselit, "The Self Readymade," *Infinite Regress: Marcel Duchamp 1910–1941* (Cambridge, MA: MIT Press, 1998), 184–193.
2   Victor Stoichita, *A Short History of the Shadow* (London: Reaktion Books, 1997), 24.
3   Otto Rank, *The Double: A Psychoanalytic Study* (Maresfield Library), trans. and ed. by Harry Tucker, Jr. (London: Karnac Books, 1989), 15.
4   Andrew J. Webber, *The Doppelganger: Double Visions in German Literature* (Oxford: Clarendon Press, 1996), 3.
5   Rank, 4.
6   Stoichita, 24.
7   Webber, 9.
8   Ibid., 4.
9   Rank, xiii.
10 Marvin Carlson, *The Haunted Stage: The Theatre as Memory Machine* (Ann Arbor: University of Michigan Press, 2003), 77.
11 Webber, 9.
12 Dietrich Scheunemann, ed., *Expressionist Film: New Perspectives* (Rochester, NY, and Melton, Suffolk: Camden House, 2006), 132.
13 Ed Lachman, quoted from Lachman's notebook and discussed with the author, New York, August 12, 2011.
14 Lachman, August 12, 2011.
15 Paul Fleming, "Tripleganger: Slater Bradley's 'Doppelganger' Trilogy," accessed September 30, 2011, http://www.blumandpoe.com, December 2005.
16 Webber, 3.
17 Stoichita, 45.
18 Ibid., 109.

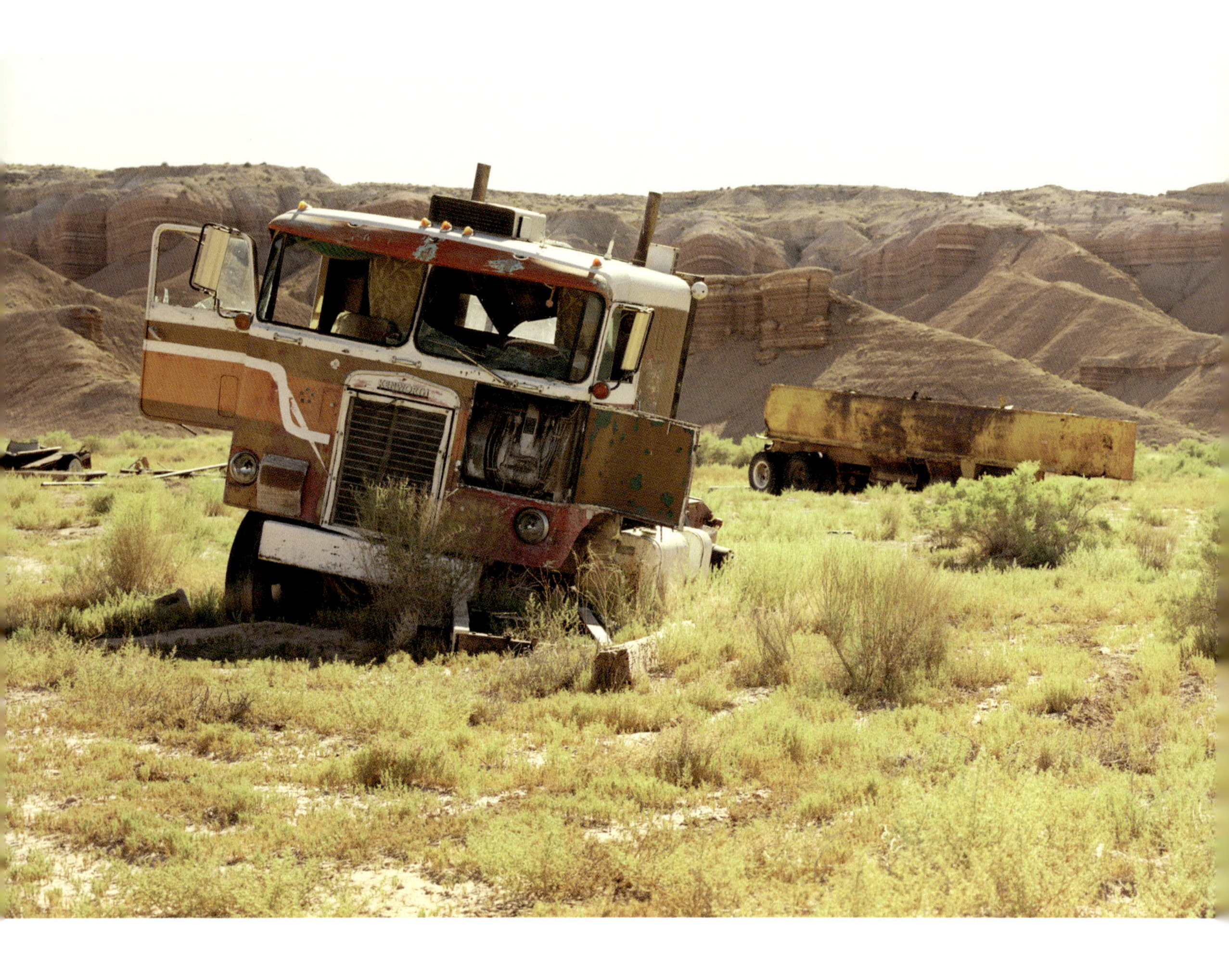

Shadow
Production Stills

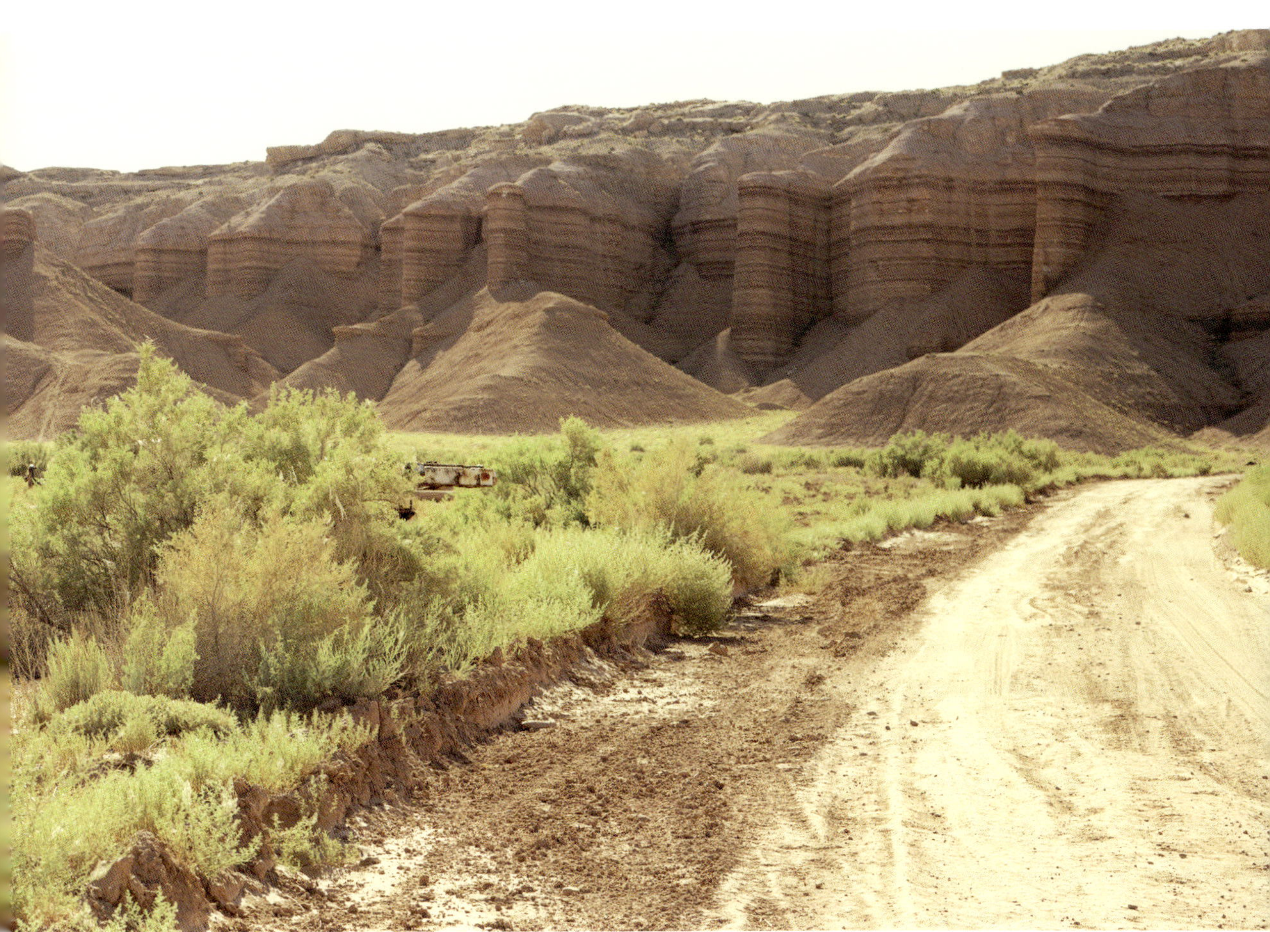

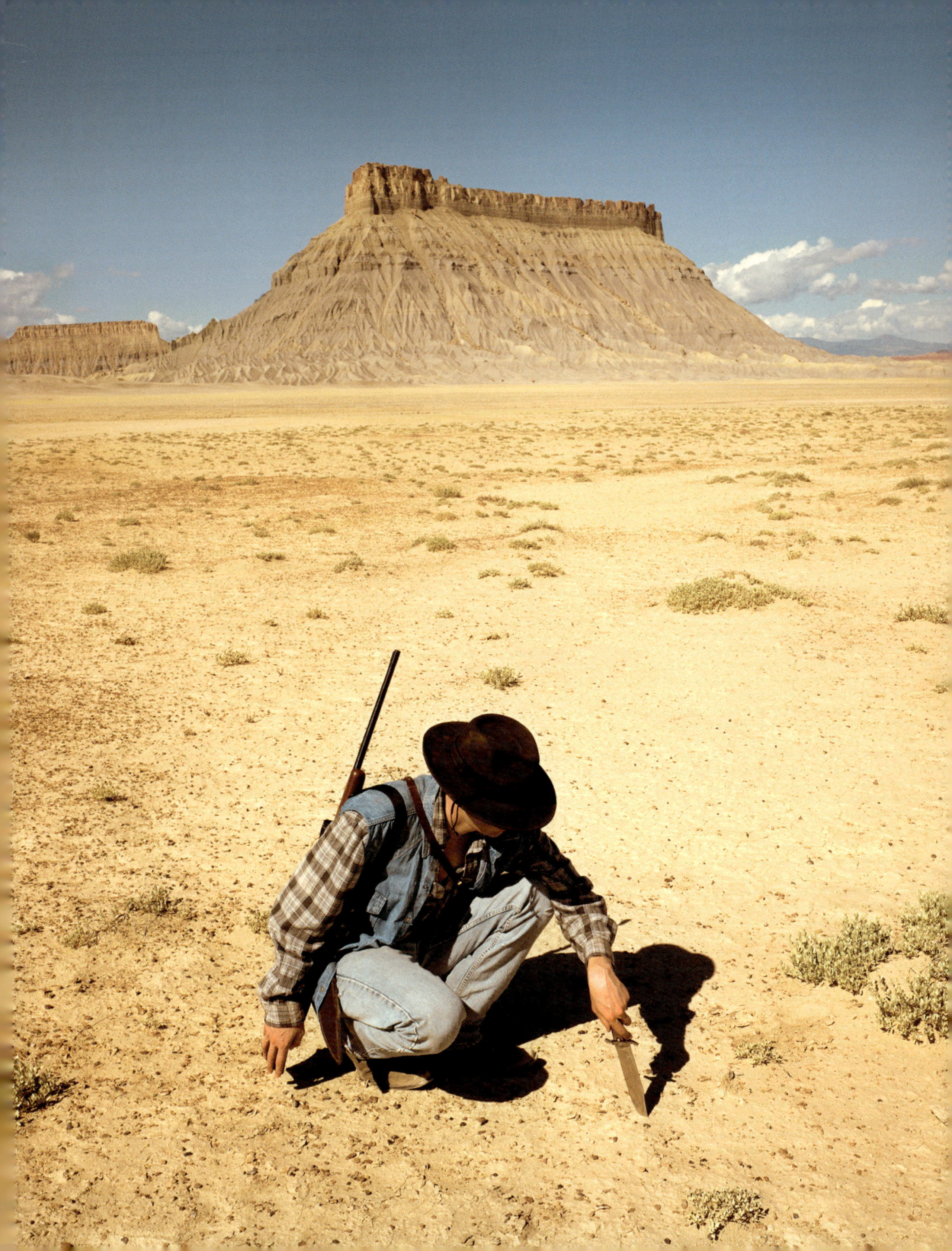

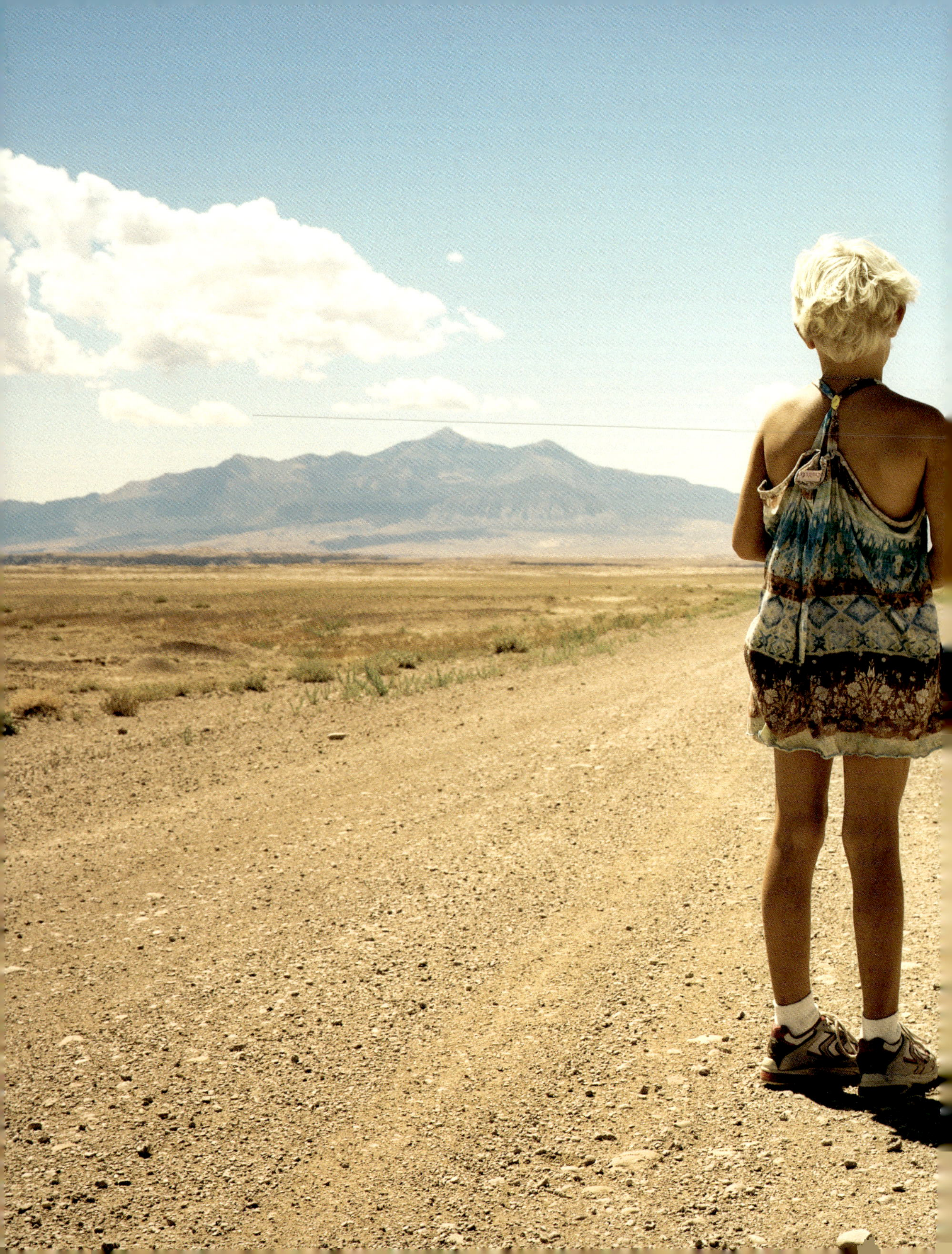

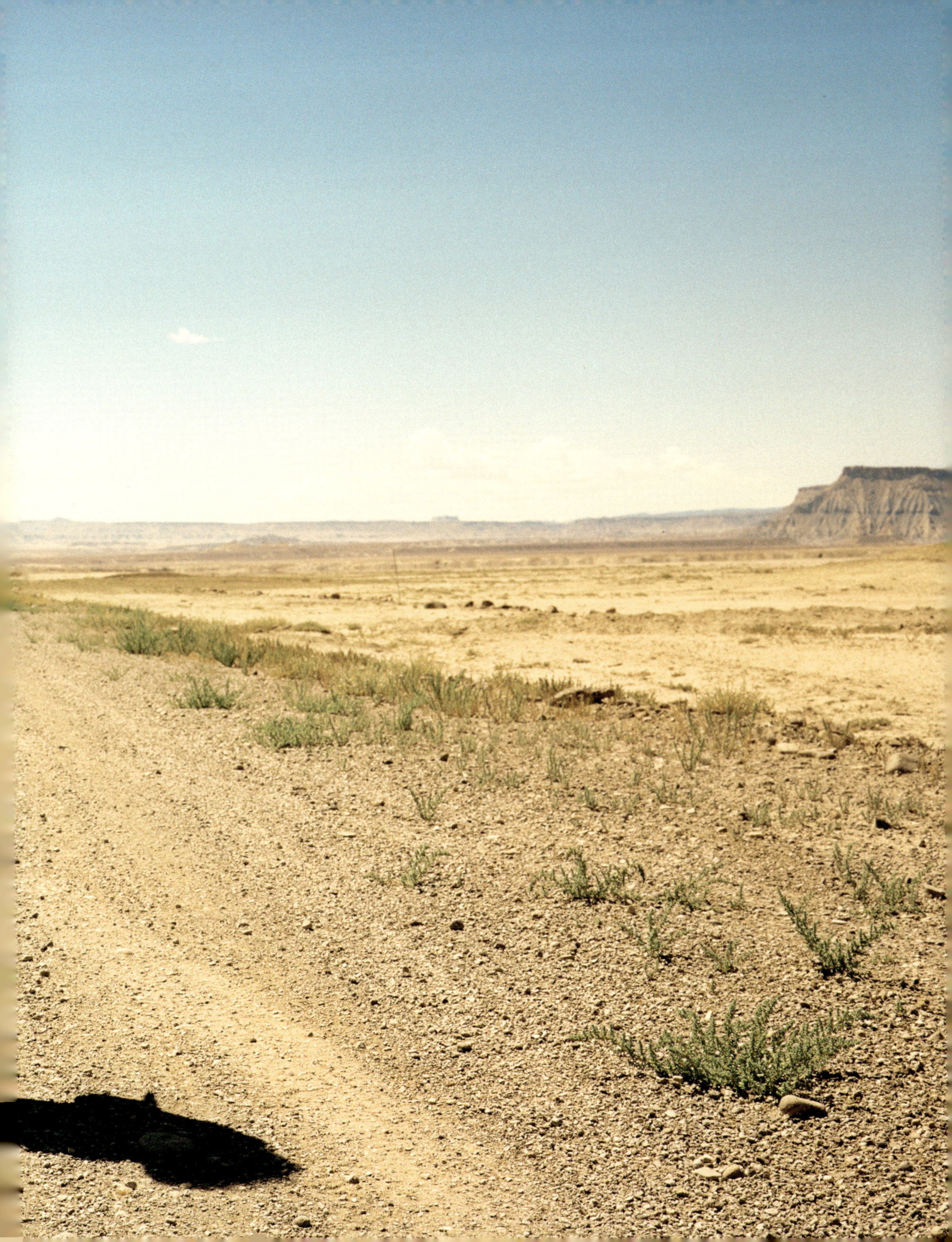

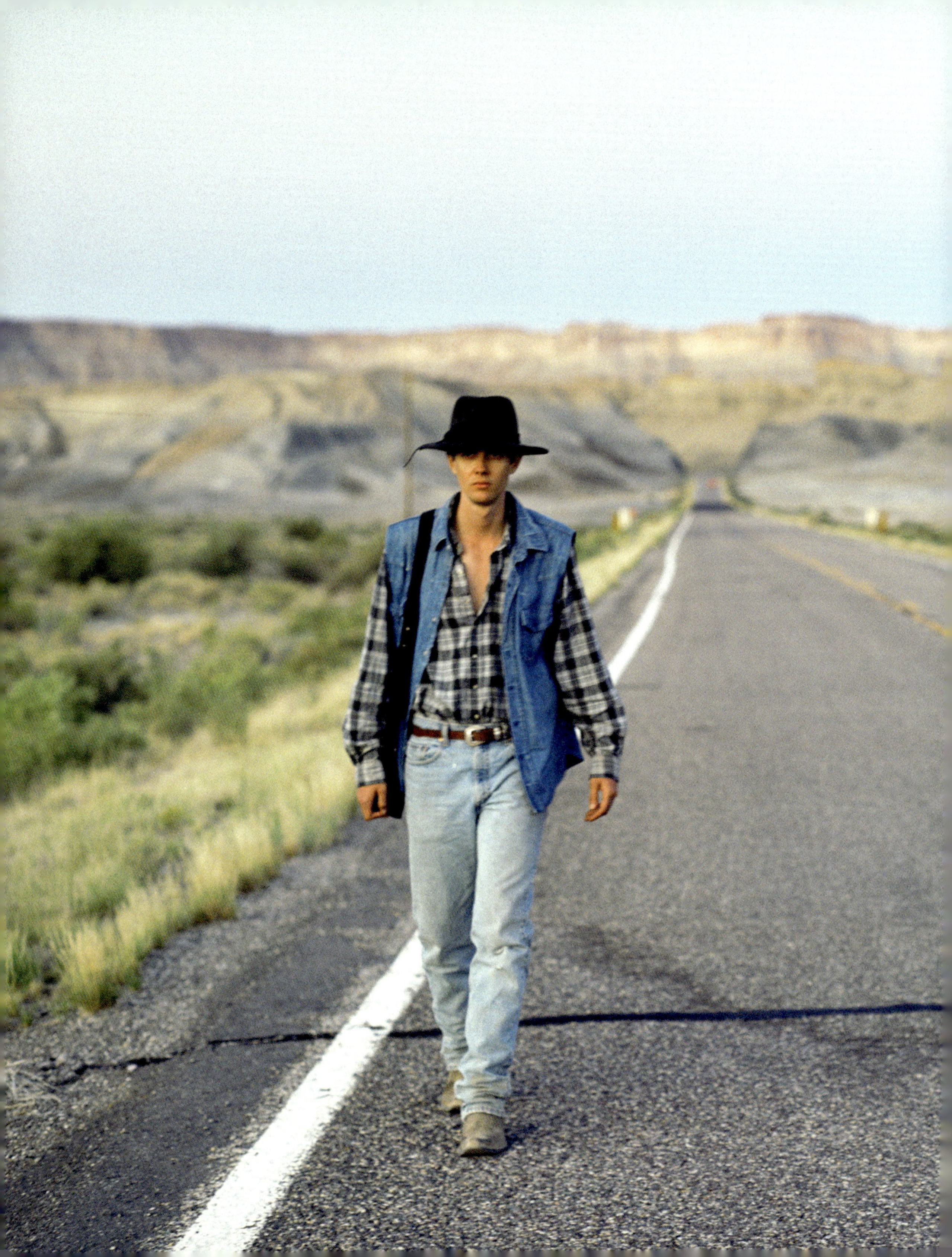

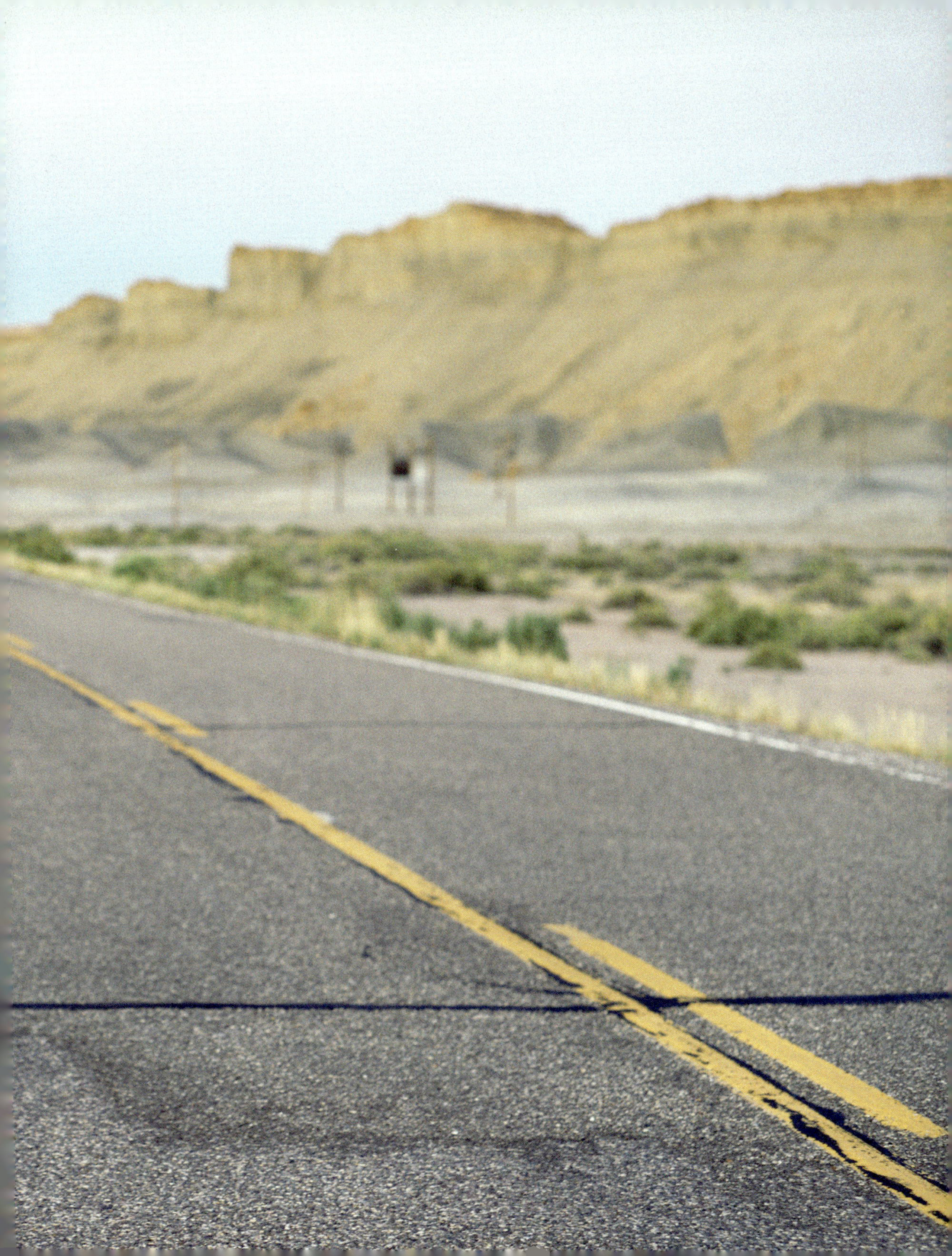

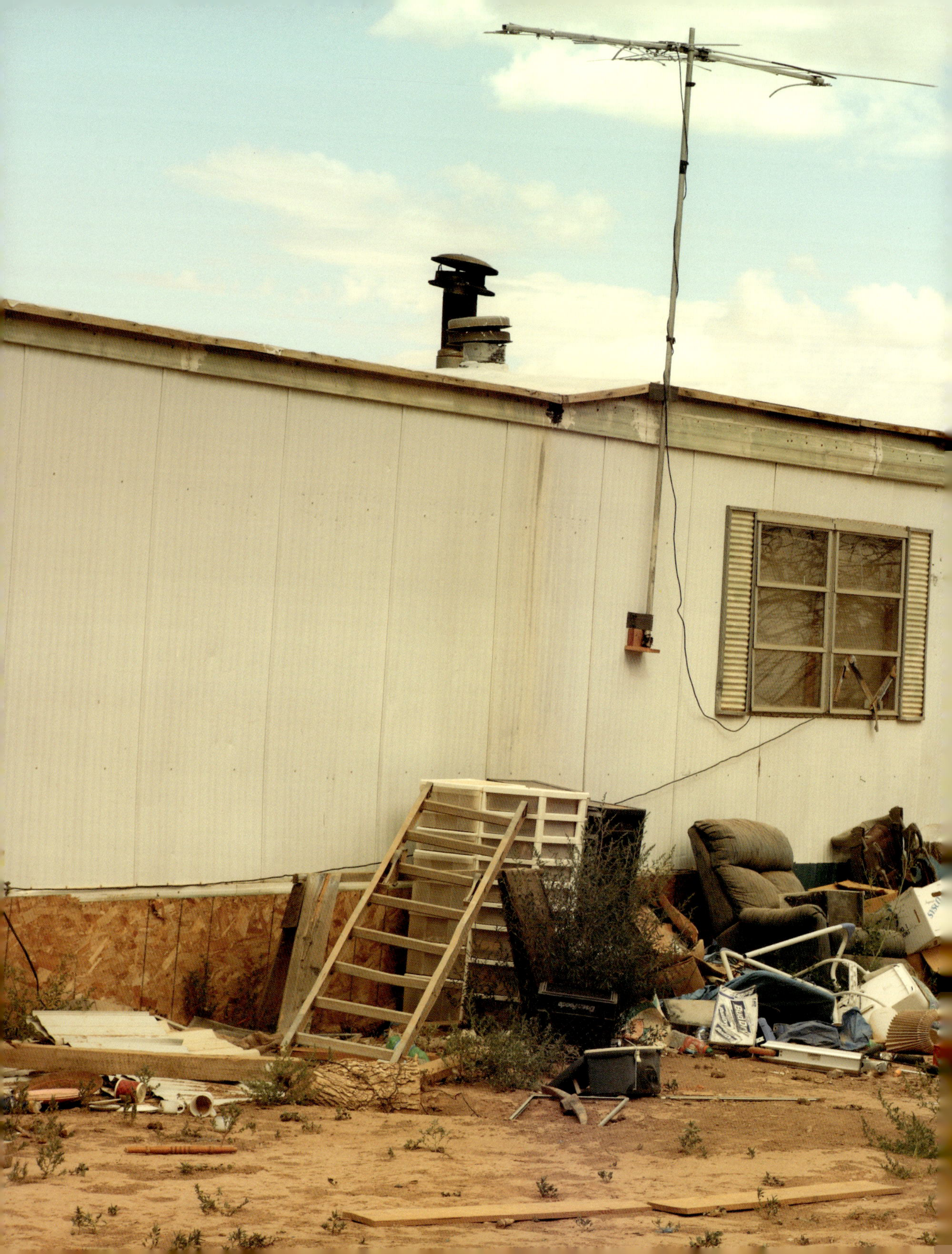

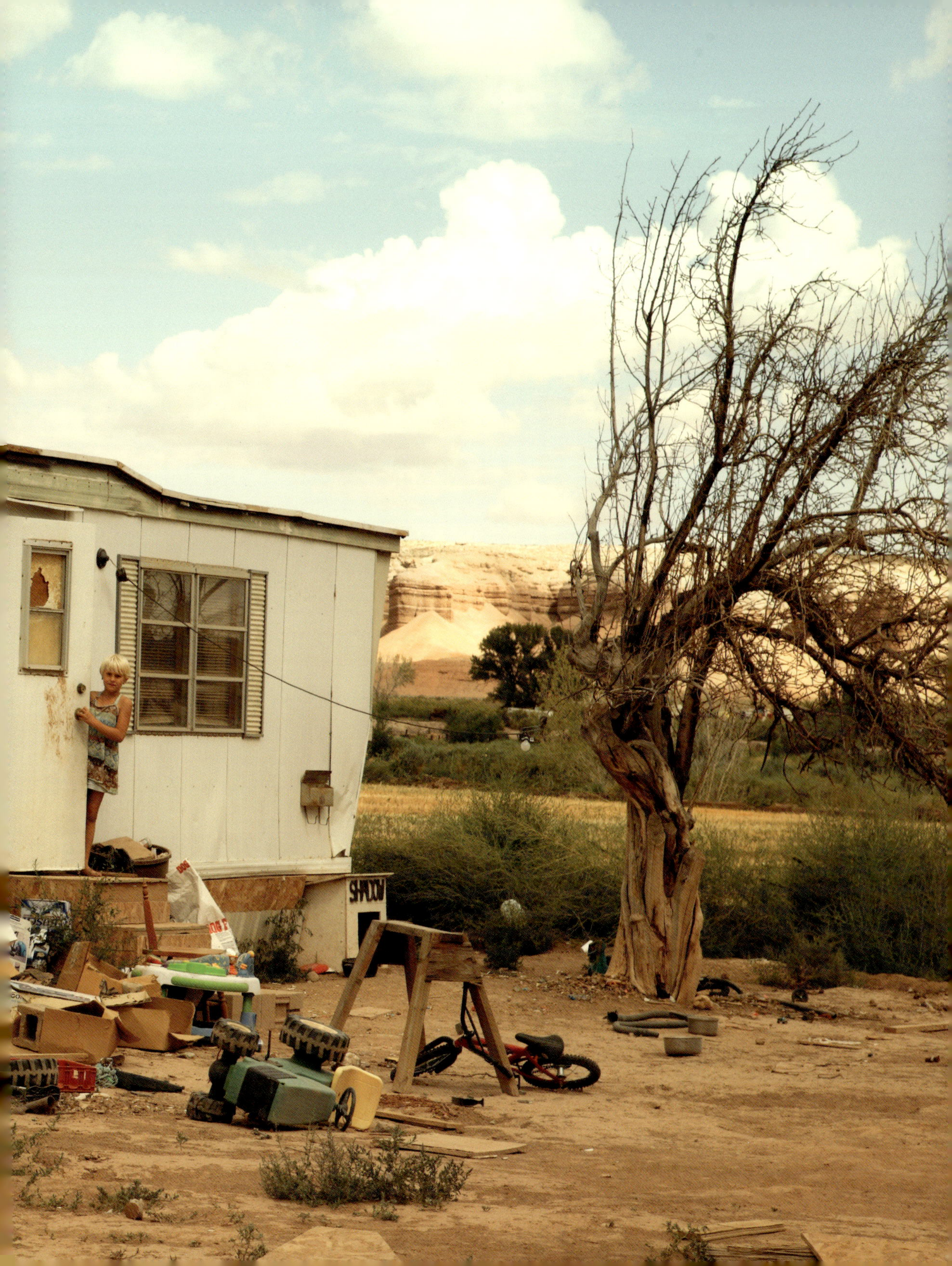
SHADOW

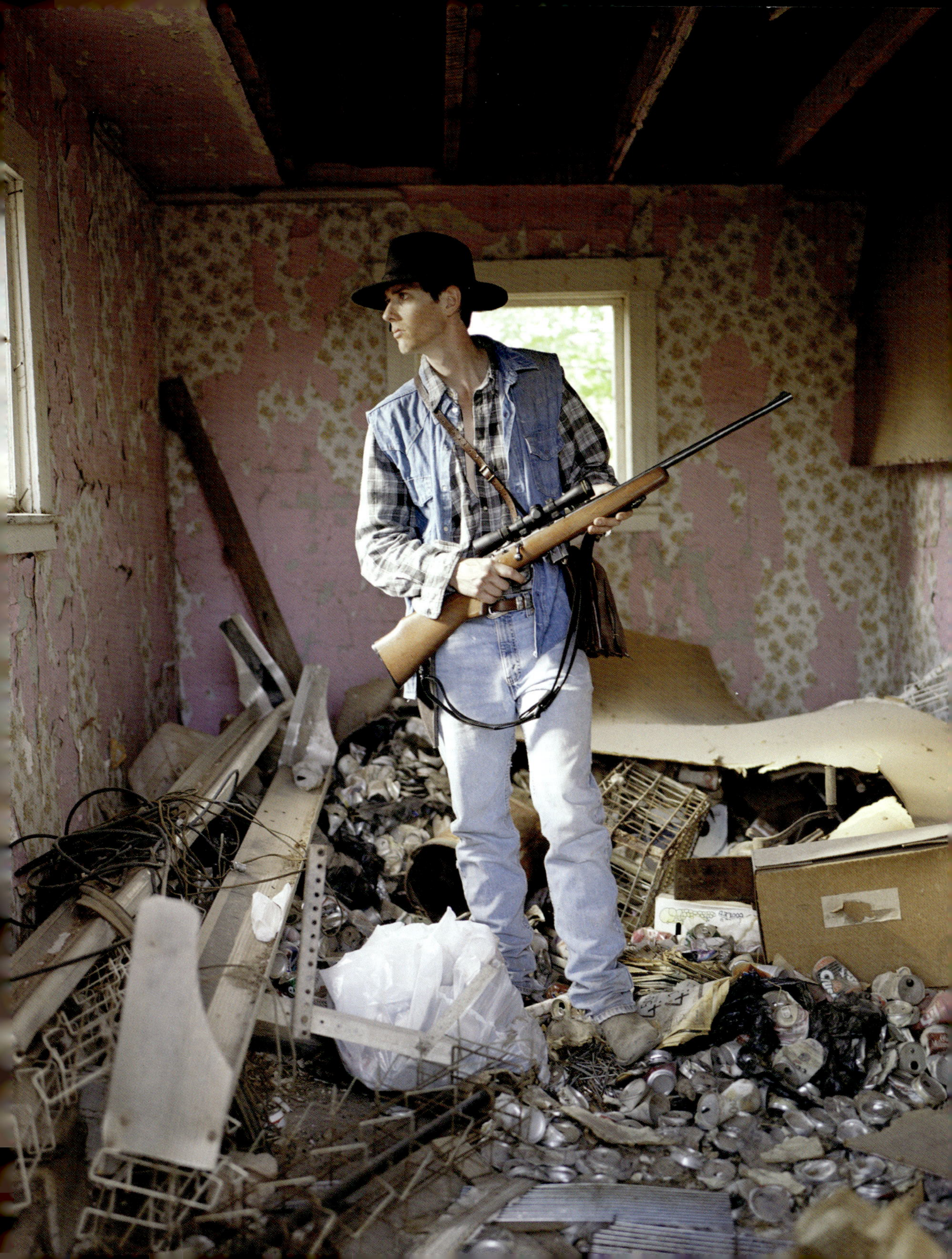

Mark Rappolt

Doppelgangers

Thanks to *Back to the Future II* (1989), everyone knows that meeting another version of yourself whilst traveling through space or time can have terrible consequences. Who could forget the wild-eyed, crazy-haired Dr. Emmett Brown, inventor of time-traveling modifications to an iconic DeLorean DMC-12, preaching the apocalyptic warning that such an encounter would do nothing less than "unravel the very fabric of the space-time continuum and destroy the entire universe?" Evidently Slater Bradley could. For more than a decade the artist has played around with his double. And, like a child's chemistry set, it's been threatening to go everywhere.

Bradley was fourteen when *Back to the Future II* was released and represented pretty precisely the movie's target demographic. Nirvana's first album, *Bleach*, was also released in 1989 and, as Bradley's work—in particular *Phantom Release* (2003), a three-minute-long "newly discovered" fan-made video of a Nirvana performance—demonstrates, the artist went on to develop a healthy obsession with that band. (*Stoned & Dethroned*, a 2004 solo exhibition at New York's Team Gallery collected *Phantom Release* and a series of photographic works based on Cobain, to mark the tenth anniversary of the singer's suicide.) Indeed, the celebrities—chief among them (besides Cobain) Joy Division's lead singer Ian Curtis, the self-styled king of pop Michael Jackson, and most recently the actor River Phoenix—around whom Bradley formulates a large part of his work were those that he encountered or that rose to prominence during the formative years of his life. So, given the extent to which his oeuvre harks back to an era that began around the late 1980s and early 1990s, an era whose cultural productions he was clearly lapping up, it's hard to argue that the juvenile Bradley's mind simply wasn't ready to take in *Back to the Future II*'s fundamental message.

Bradley first encountered his own double, a man called Ben Brock, in various nightclubs during the late 1990s. Bradley and Brock look and act uncannily alike. Back then people kept telling the artist that they had seen him at places he was not. Creepy. But instead of keeping apart, like Dr. Brown ordered, they began to work together, with Bradley first casting Brock in one of his works late in 1999. Not long afterwards, Bradley's college roommate spent ten minutes talking to Brock in a nightclub before realizing he'd got the wrong man. "I guess that was the moment I knew that this project had legs," the artist says, also recalling—as if to up both the creepiness and the sense that he's ignoring some obvious signs and portents—how, on the only occasion that he visited Brock's house in Ohio, all the plates in the kitchen fell off their shelves as soon as Bradley crossed the threshold.[1]

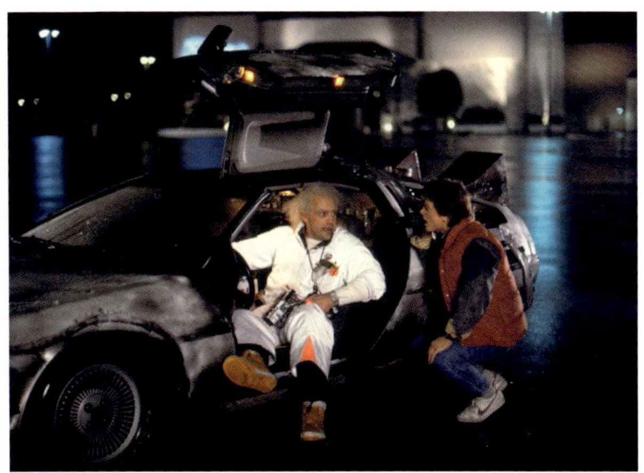

Christopher Lloyd as Dr. Emmett Brown (center) in *Back to the Future* (Robert Zemeckis, 1985).

The relationship was affirmed at *Charlatan*, a 2000 exhibition at Team, when Bradley began passing off photographs of Brock as if they were portraits of the artist himself.

Using the kind of literary terminology the *Back to the Future* franchise by and large eschews, Bradley refers to his other as a "doppelganger," a word that first emerged in nineteenth-century German literature to describe a particular kind of ghoul that replicated the person of the individual it visited and that has since been co-opted into English to mean a double in a more general sense. Nevertheless, like the potential encounters with past or future selves in *Back to the Future II*, the appearance of a doppelganger is traditionally bad news. It's a bringer of ill tidings. An omen of death. The sinister stuff of bad dreams and nightmares. The nasty Mr. Hyde to one's nice Dr. Jekyll. Legend has it that the poet Percy Bysshe Shelley had visions in which he encountered a copy of himself issuing ominous warnings shortly before he drowned; John Donne is said to have had a similar nightmare before his wife miscarried; in literature the doppelganger can be found, in various guises, in the works of Poe, Hoffmann, Andersen, Dostoyevsky, Gogol, Melville, Conrad, and Mann, to name just a few. In fact, such was its ubiquity in turn-of-the-century literature that when questioned, in 1966, about themes of the double in his own work—most prominently *Lolita* (1955), an annotated edition of which Bradley had been reading shortly before his first encounter with Brock, and *Pale Fire* (1962)—Vladimir Nabokov would declare that "the doppelganger subject is a frightful bore."[2]

Clearly Bradley begs to differ. Brock appears in the three videos that make up the artist's much-lauded *Doppelganger Trilogy*, a series of works that explores the mechanics of celebrity and identity formation in a fully mediated (perhaps even more specifically Internet) age. The trilogy comprises *Factory Archives* (2001–2), in which Brock channels Ian Curtis; the previously mentioned *Phantom Release,* in which it is Brock who plays Cobain; and *Recorded Yesterday* (2004), in which

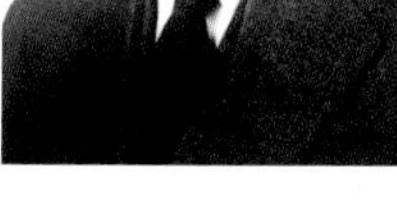

Vladimir Nabokov

You just split

Brock performs as Michael Jackson moonwalking. More recently, Brock has appeared again in *Dark Night of the Soul* (2005–6), during which the actor, safely encased within an astronaut's suit, wanders around New York's American Museum of Natural History to the accompaniment of Beethoven's "Moonlight Sonata," and *Boulevard of broken dreams* (2009), in which a seemingly alienated Brock embarks on a moody stroll through

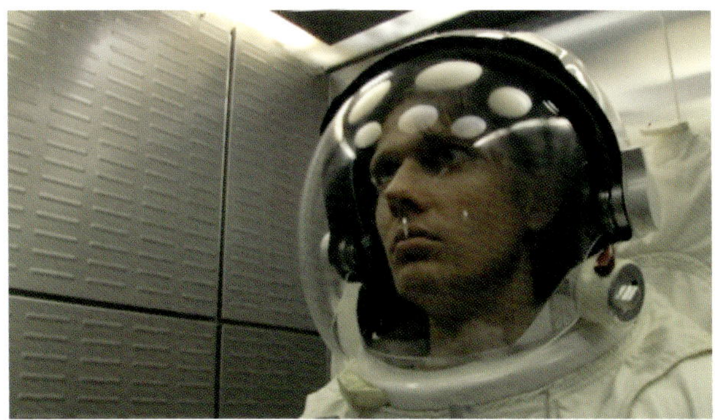

Slater Bradley, *Dark Night of the Soul*, 2005/06.

Manhattan, evoking J. D. Salinger's *Catcher in the Rye* (1951) and invoking occasional lines from M. Ageyev's *Novel with Cocaine* (1934). In a funny way it's as if the Brock of *Dark Night of the Soul* forgot to take his spacesuit off for *Boulevard of broken dreams*.

And yet, despite all that, on the evidence of his latest video work, coauthored by filmmaker Ed Lachman, there are signs that even Bradley may have had enough of all this doubling up. In *Dead Ringer* (2011), a three-channel looped video, the artist appears to have split Brock's head open with an axe.

my head open

"You just split my head open," says Brock disbelievingly as he uncertainly picks himself up off the ground. "I've never wanted to kill a man before," he continues, shakily aiming his rifle towards the camera (and the general direction from which Bradley will later emerge) before collapsing in a heap. Even his final words seem to be spoken on Bradley's behalf. And while all this may not be quite the apocalypse Dr. Brown envisaged (and given that Brock and Bradley are only on screen at the same time when one of them is dead, it's far from clear whether or not this is an incident Brown would worry about), in the context of Bradley's oeuvre, his scuttle from one side of the camera to the other nevertheless appears to mark a turning point.

Dead Ringer is based, like the artist's related video *Shadow* (2010), on scenes from *Dark Blood*, a feature film directed by George Sluizer but left unfinished and unreleased following the death of its star, River Phoenix,

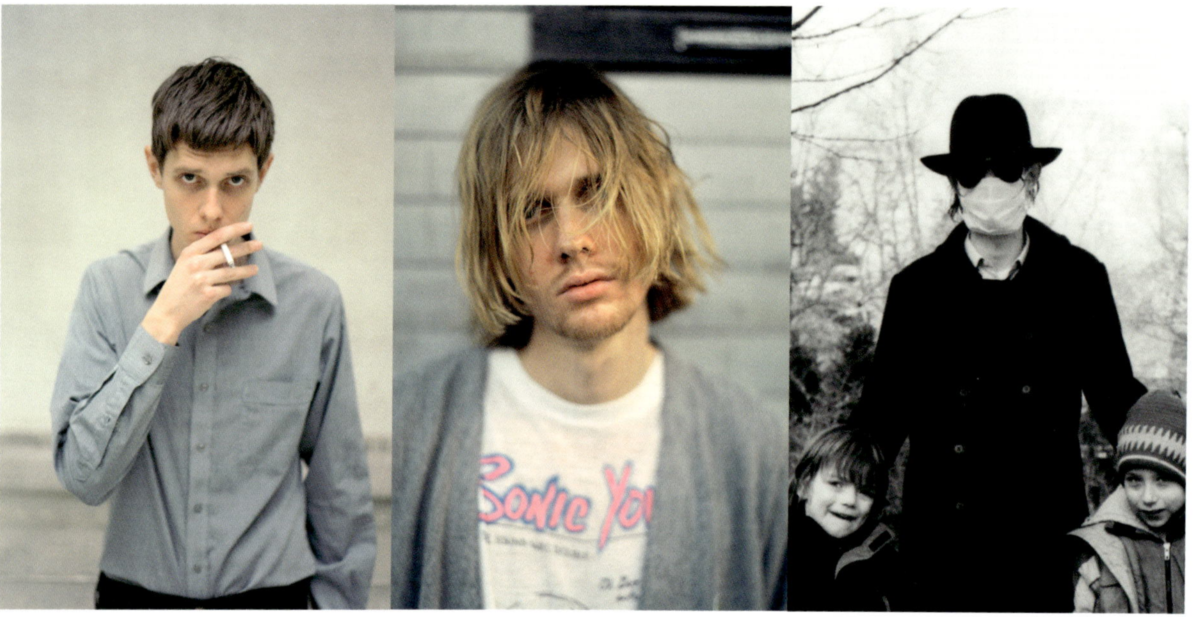

The Doppelganger as Ian Curtis, Kurt Cobain, and Michael Jackson in Slater Bradley's *Factory Ikon*, 2000/04 (left); *I hate myself and want to die*, 2003/04 (center); and *The Animals (outtake)*, 2004 (right).

outside West Hollywood's Viper Room after a drug overdose in 1993.[3] Coincidentally, but apparently confirming 1989 as a foundational year in Bradley's life, Phoenix's appearance as the young Indy in the movie *Indiana Jones and the Last Crusade* (1989) was, according to the artist, an experience that cemented his interest in the subsequently doomed actor.[4] You can see Phoenix performing the scene performed by Brock in *Dead Ringer* on one of the few clips from *Dark Blood* that's escaped onto YouTube. Indeed, it's not just that you can; you're expected to. As I write this, 91,798 other people already have.[5] And aside from Bradley popping into the final frames of *Dead*

Ringer to claim the kill (and his hat), the artwork is a relatively faithful replica of the original clip (Phoenix's character dies in the original movie).

The direction towards this kind of source material—YouTube fragments, fan-released material—is a crucial component of Bradley's work. In part that's because the fan networks on which such clips generally appear are one of the subjects of his art. But it's also important because, on a fundamental level, Bradley's work is not even aimed at an art audience. After all, unless the members of that audience are fans of the stars, they most probably couldn't care less whether or not Brock's words in *Dead Ringer* are indeed the same as those spoken by Phoenix (they are), or that Brock, like Cobain, is left-handed and therefore plays guitar in the same direction. Indeed, even if that audience did care they'd need to resort to an Internet search rather than anything the artist provides in his exhibitions to test the authenticity of such works. In short, Bradley's works turn on the assumption that you know where they're coming from. And that, rather than any test, is what gives them the feel of authenticity upon which their reception (both as brilliant fakes or as potentially authentic footage) depends.

At a fundamental level, the work is aimed at someone who might appreciate all the details. "I copied Nirvana's instruments and clothes," Bradley wrote of *Phantom Release*, "so that even the most hardcore fan would not be disappointed by a dumb mistake in detail."[6] So it's the hardcore fan, apparently, that Bradley seeks to please. As much as Brock performs to double the artist and to double the stars that are the ostensible subjects of Bradley's work, Bradley doubles the subcultures of fandom. Perhaps he doesn't even go so far as to double it. Given that the celebrities he and Brock conjure are important influences on Bradley's life, perhaps he is actually operating as nothing more than a fan. And yet this very uncertainty—the fact that Bradley may not actually have

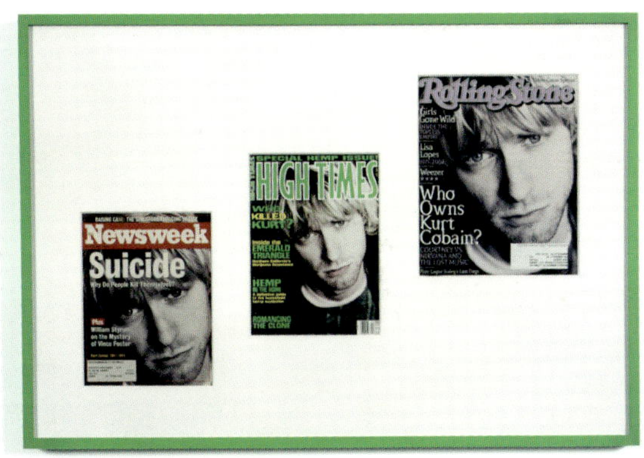

Slater Bradley, *Marijuana*, 2004.

the kind of distance we expect of an artist when they're offering a critique of a particular culture, that far from critiquing it he may simply be reveling in it—is part of the thrill of looking at his work.

Phantom Release was in part inspired by the digitalnirvana.net website on which fans trade information about bootlegs and unofficial recordings of the band. Writing about the work (to accompany a 2004 exhibition of *The Doppelganger Trilogy* at Blum & Poe in Los Angeles) Bradley recalls that he wanted to create an equivalent to the Super 8 footage that might have been lost and found in a fan's basement, just as he had found the collection of 1994 obituary magazines he had stored in a basement to use as source material when it came to creating the *Stoned & Dethroned* show. And perhaps this is why our old friend Dr. Brown might not need to be so worried about Bradley messing around with Brock—it's far from clear whether Brock's doubling Curtis, Cobain, Jackson, Phoenix, or Bradley, or all of the above. Perhaps, even, Brock's presence as an interface between the artist and celebrity subject suggests that the relationship between the famous and the fan is so complete that it's impossible to identify which is which: the one is simply a prosthesis appended to the other. It's like watching a set of Fibonacci numbers unfold and then collapse before your eyes. And, of course, you're implicitly invited to test the logic of their sequencing.

There is indeed, in Bradley's work, some suggestion of equivalence between the person who views Bradley's engagement with celebrity from the perspective of a fan and the person who views it as an artwork. For the art person, just as for the fan, there's the titillation of voyeurism. For the fan it comes about through seeking to know the habits, rituals, and routines—what food they eat, where they hang out, where they shop, etc.—of the object of their attention so completely that it, perversely, strips the celebrity of anything that made them special (thus allowing the fan further to identify with them). For the art person it comes via the thrill of peeking into the world of someone else's obsession, combined with a desire to find some sort of universal, communicable truth in the work (like I'm doing now), a kind of knowledge (in Bradley's case, this tends to be some sort of understanding of the sociopolitical aspects of celebrity in the Internet age) that binds them to fellow art aficionados just as surely as the knowledge that Kurt Cobain was left-handed does when it comes to identifying a community of "true" Nirvana fans. And just as that sinistral knowledge allows the true Nirvana fan to look down upon the fan who doesn't know (allowing them to exclude the ignoramus from the community of true fans), so the ability to extract a "higher" reading, beyond the mere glitz of celebrity, separates the community of art experts from art amateurs.

At the heart of the relationship between fandom and the object of its adulation is a sense of community, or, depending on your politics, even an erotics or commodity exchange (love being the commodity). It's one that's best described by a celebrity, in this case Nikki Sixx, Mötley Crüe's bass player. Recalling his thoughts on a drive home from the hospital after he had been admitted following a drug overdose and subsequently reported dead on local radio: "I felt so alone and monstrous on tour, as if I had nobody that cared for me and nobody to care for. In that car, I realized that I was one of the luckiest guys in the world. I had millions of people who cared for me and millions of people I cared for."[7]

Of course, for anyone outside the bubble of mutual appreciation Sixx describes, it's almost impossible to read the musician's words and not think that Sixx is somewhat delusional, probably prone to exaggeration, and certainly narcissistic. But all that does highlight the Gulliverian sense of scale of the celebrity-fan relationship: on the one hand, there's the fan's microscopic attention to the details of their heroes' lives, and on the other, the celebrity's expectation that such details have a lasting appeal to a wide audience. And both of these perspectives play out in Bradley's work: on the one hand his insistence on exact verisimilitude, and on the other the belief, implicit in the very act of offering his work up for public scrutiny, that his subject matter will appeal to a wider audience than that of the mere fan. This can be both horrifying—in Jonathan Swift's 1726 novel Gulliver gets washed up in Brobdingnag, where he gets to see people twelve times his size in such microscopic detail, to the pores of their skin and the hairs on a lady's nipple, that he is eventually disgusted rather than awed by them—and revelatory—in Lilliput, where Gulliver is twelve times the size of the average inhabitant, he learns that being big and powerful doesn't make life's problems any smaller. Everyone, the story of Gulliver tells us, is horribly and disgustingly the same.

In the end Bradley is less interested in people like Sixx and more interested in celebrities who couldn't handle their fame and did die of depression (Curtis and Cobain are suicides) or overindulgence (while Jackson died some time after Bradley made *Recorded Yesterday*, the artist has stated that the appeal of the subject lay in the singer's gradual withdrawal from public life),[8] which makes Brock–Phoenix's violent demise in the aptly named *Dead Ringer* even more of a tease. Who the hell is Brock in this work? Is he doing nothing more than simply acting out one of Phoenix's scenes? Just being Phoenix? Or does his demise and Bradley's emergence signal the end of the latter's reliance of the former?

Both *Shadow* and *Dead Ringer* were created in collaboration with filmmaker Ed Lachman, the actual cinematographer on *Dark Blood* seventeen years ago. *Shadow* and *Dead Ringer* each star Brock in the role of Phoenix as channeled by Lachman via his memories of the original shoot. Or, to put it another way, Lachman channels his memories, thoughts, and feelings on River Phoenix and shares them with Bradley, who then reincarnates Phoenix through Brock. In the case of *Shadow*, the result is a sort of prologue to *Dark Blood*, focusing on the Phoenix character (a reclusive widower who lives near a nuclear testing site in the Nevada desert, his wife having died of radiation poisoning) as he rambles, looking for what is lost around the original location. But *Shadow* also includes many episodes (the appearance of a mysterious young girl; an episode in Phoenix's favorite local bar) that are unrelated to the original film, but connect previous works to present fact and past fiction.

But this of course is what any memory or memorial is. Bradley states that he was inspired to contact Lachman having seen a 2006 documentary (*Final 24: River Phoenix*) that traced the final day of Phoenix's life. In it, Lachman recalls the last day of shooting on *Dark Blood*: "We did four takes of a soliloquy, the last day we shot with him on *Dark Blood*. It was in the cave on a set in Los Angeles that we had created after coming back from the desert in Utah… it was lighted to feel like it was all lit by candles. That was on Saturday—just hours before he died in front of the Viper Room early Halloween morning. When we saw the dailies on Monday morning, after the last take and we heard 'cut,' the camera was still rolling, and I realized that I hadn't turned the camera off. The lights on the set were dimmed down and for at least fifteen seconds, which seemed like a lifetime. River was standing in front of the camera as a perfect silhouette only lit by the candles. It was the eeriest feeling I've ever had with something that I had photographed. People were crying. We knew it was the last time we would ever see River."[9] What Lachman does—looking for signs and portents in the footage of Phoenix—is exactly what fans do when they pour over videos of their heroes and exactly what Bradley is asking his audience to do when confronted by his artworks.

"It's tough having heroes," the rock critic Lester Bangs once whined. "It's the hardest thing in the world. It's harder than being a hero. Heroes are generally expected to produce something or other to reconfirm their mandarin-fingered clinch on the hot buns of the bitch muse… But hero-worshippers (fans) must live with the continually confirmed dread of hero-slippage."[10] It's a dread that Bradley at once confronts—by preserving his heroes—and denies, as everything and everyone slides into one. Brock is Phoenix, is Bradley, is us, is a fan, is an art lover, is a memory, is a coconspirator, is a friend. Slippage is everywhere, from the formation of our identities to the architectures of our cultures and subcultures. Perhaps that's exactly the kind of space-time unraveling that Dr. Emmett Brown so hysterically feared back in 1989.

1   Slater Bradley, correspondence with the author, August 9, 2011.
2   Vladimir Nabokov, *Strong Opinions* (New York: Vintage, 1990), 83.
3   The footage of *Dark Blood* is currently locked in a lab due to a continuing lawsuit.
4   Bradley, August 9, 2011.
5   Slater Bradley, correspondence with the author, August 6, 2011.
6   Slater Bradley, "Slater Bradley on the *Doppelganger Trilogy*," statement accompanying the exhibition *The Doppelganger Trilogy*, Blum & Poe, Los Angeles, December 11, 2004–January 22, 2005.
7   Mötley Crüe, *The Dirt: Confessions of the Word's Most Notorious Rock Band* (New York: Harper Entertainment, 2001), 207.
8   Bradley, August 9, 2011.
9   Ed Lachman, correspondence with the author, September 27, 2011.
10 Lester Bangs, 'David Bowie: Station to Station', *Psychotic Reactions and Carburetor Dung*, (London: Serpent's Tail, 1996), 161.

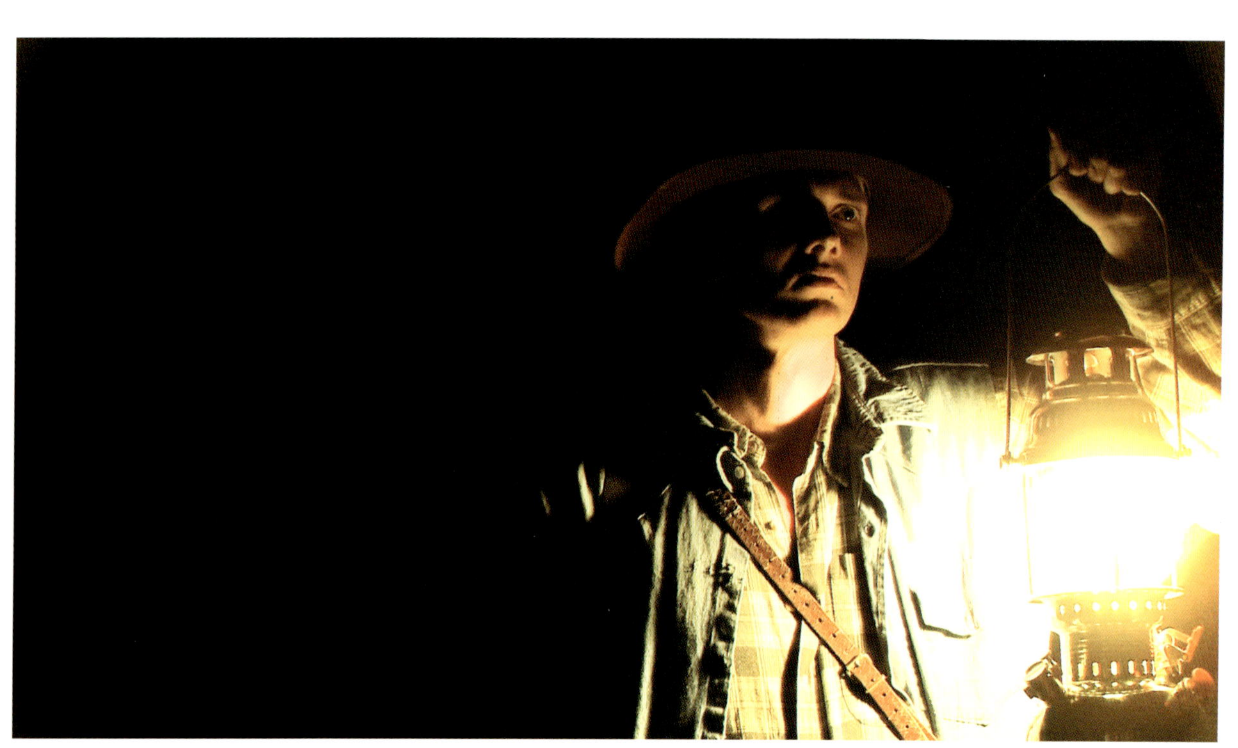

Shadow

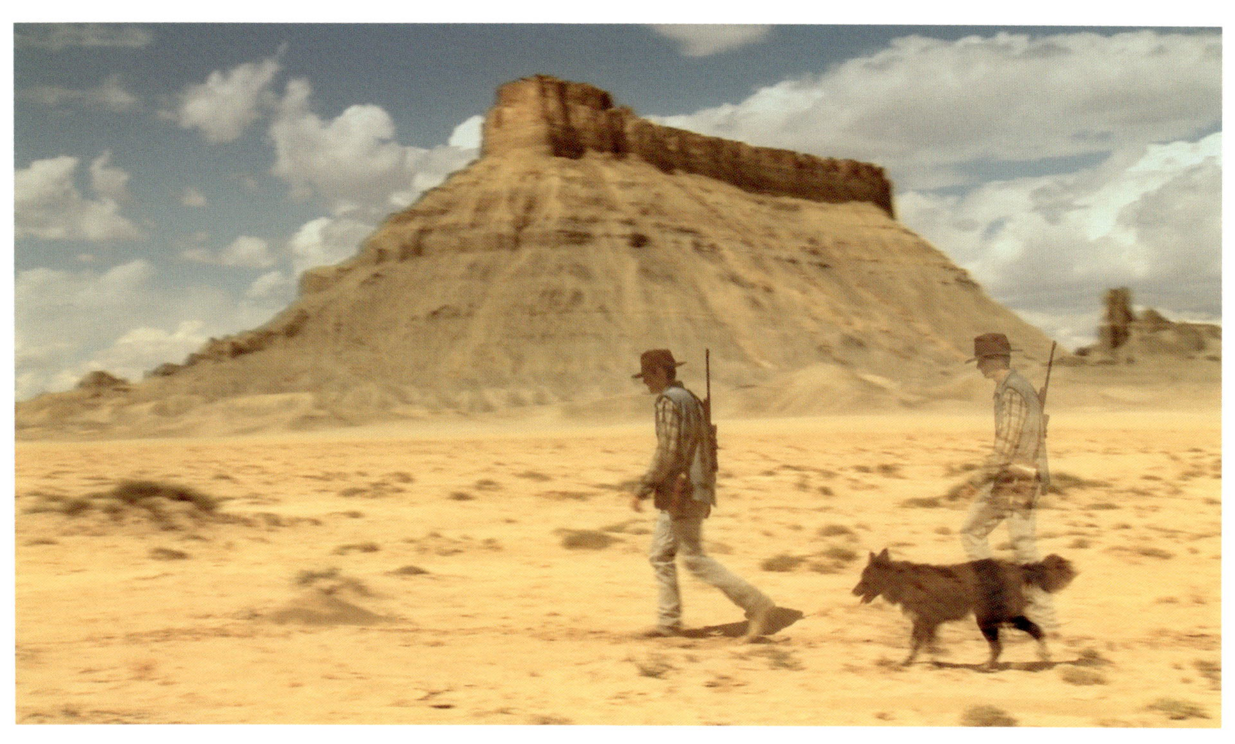

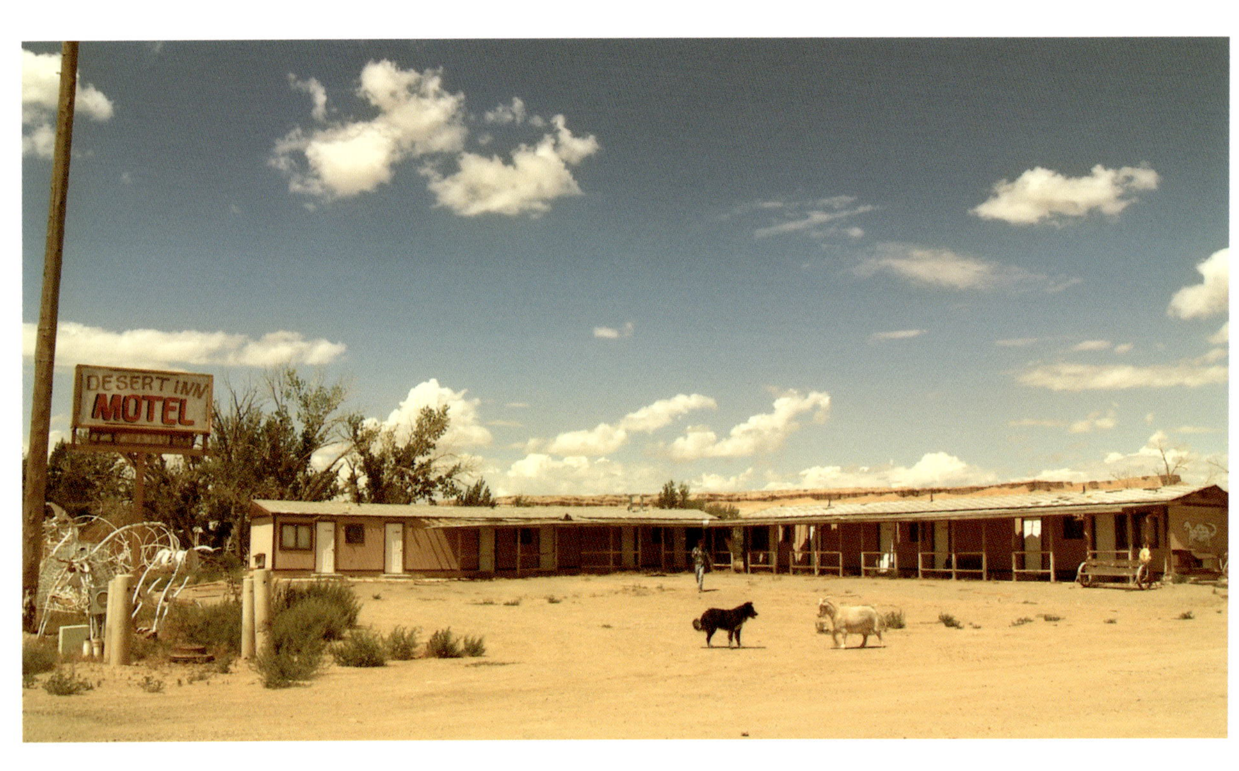
DESERT INN
MOTEL

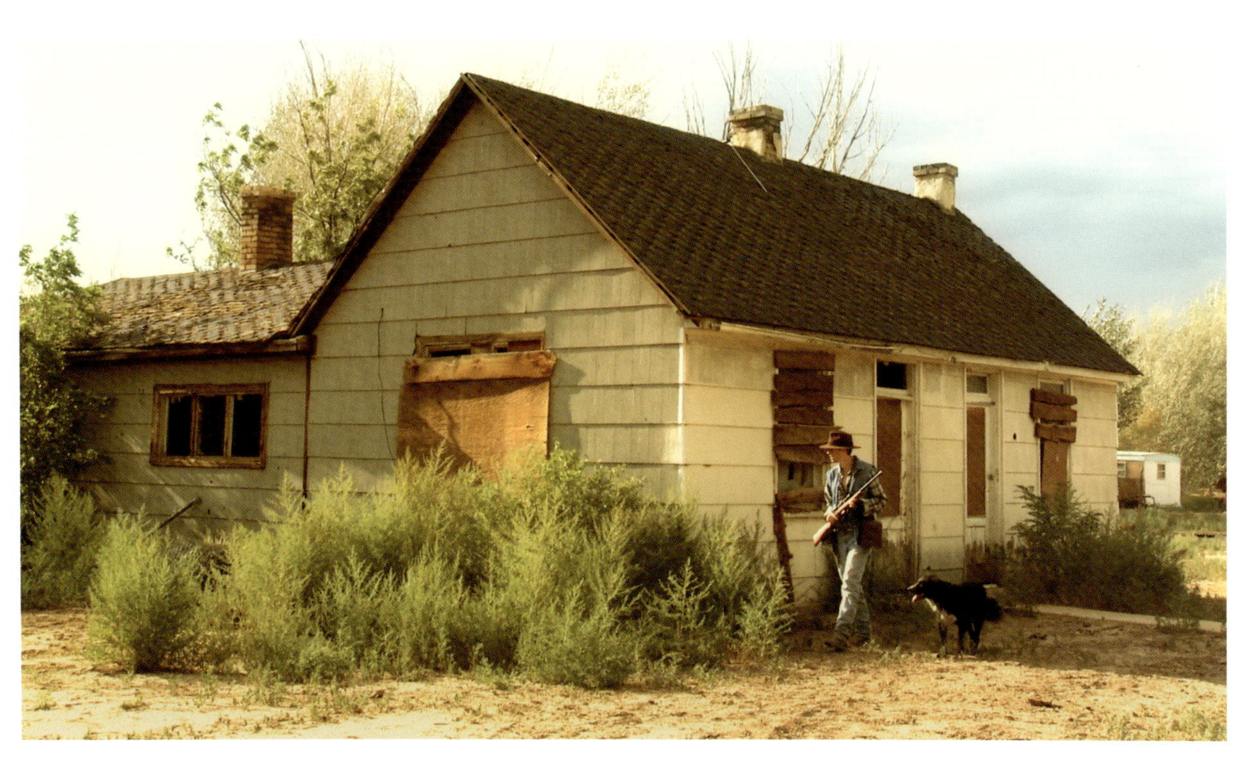

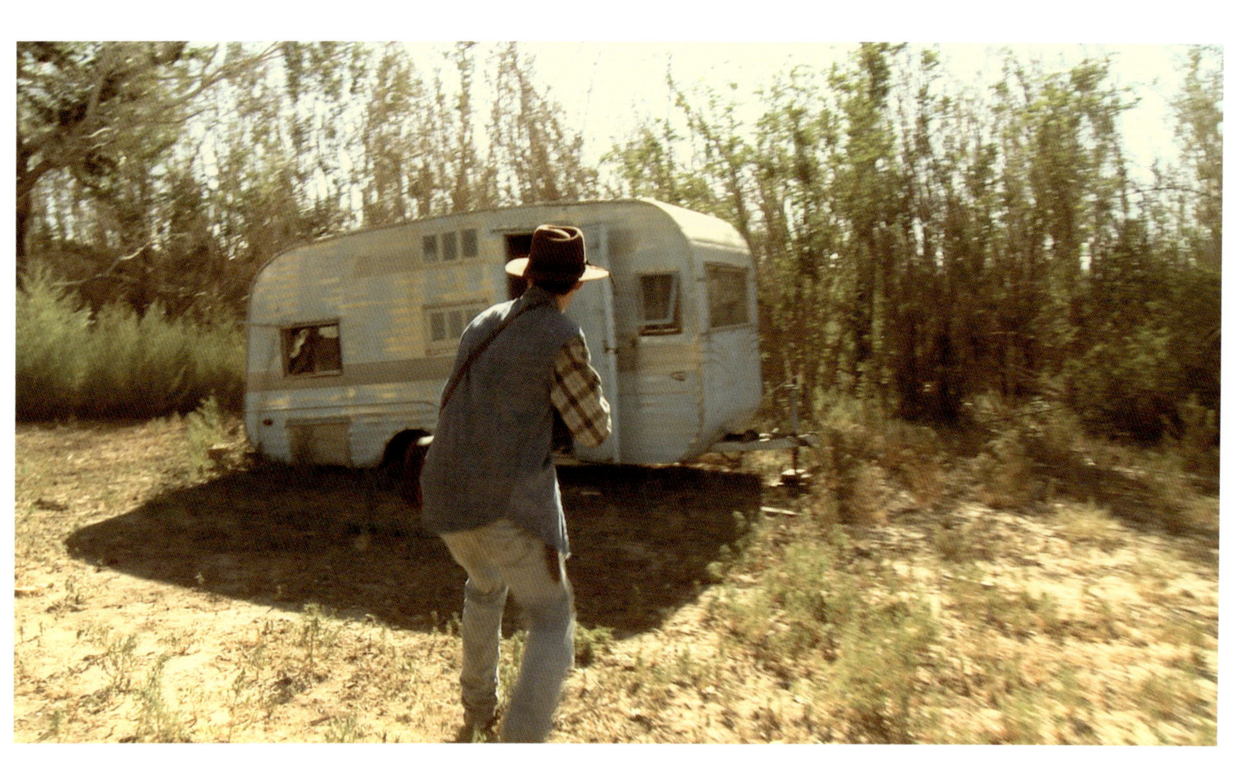

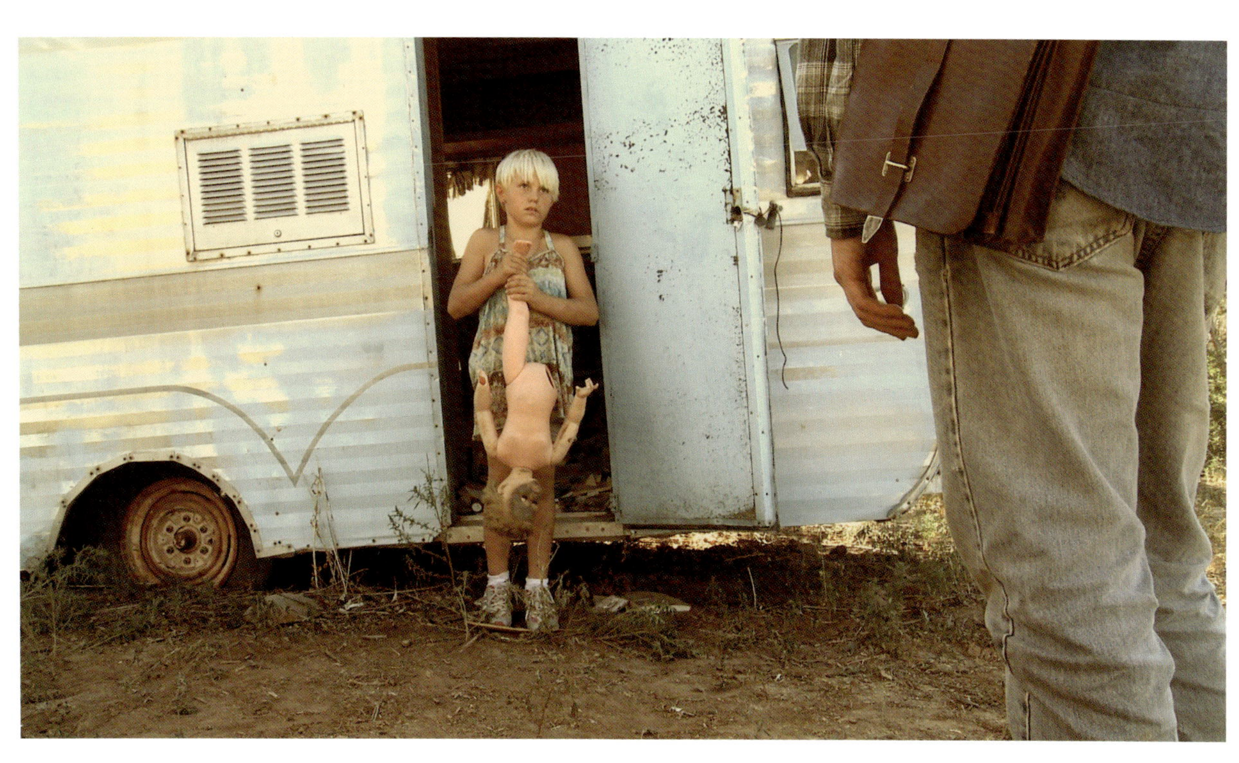

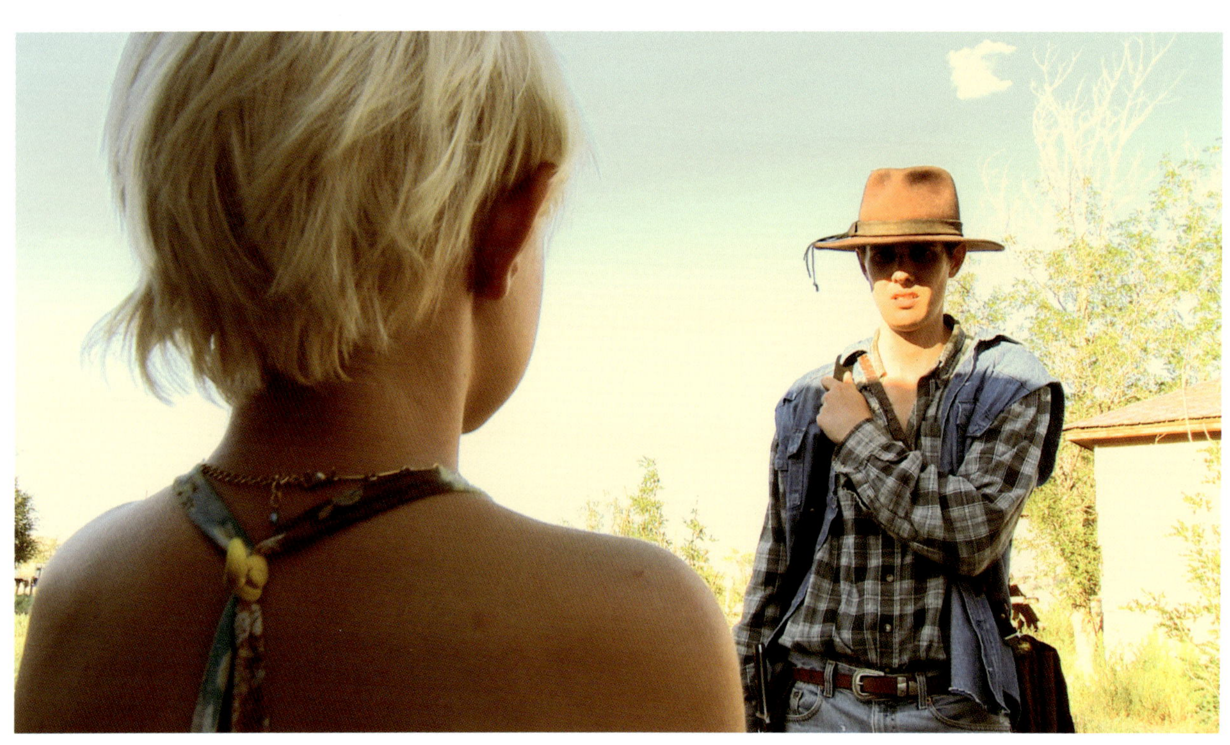

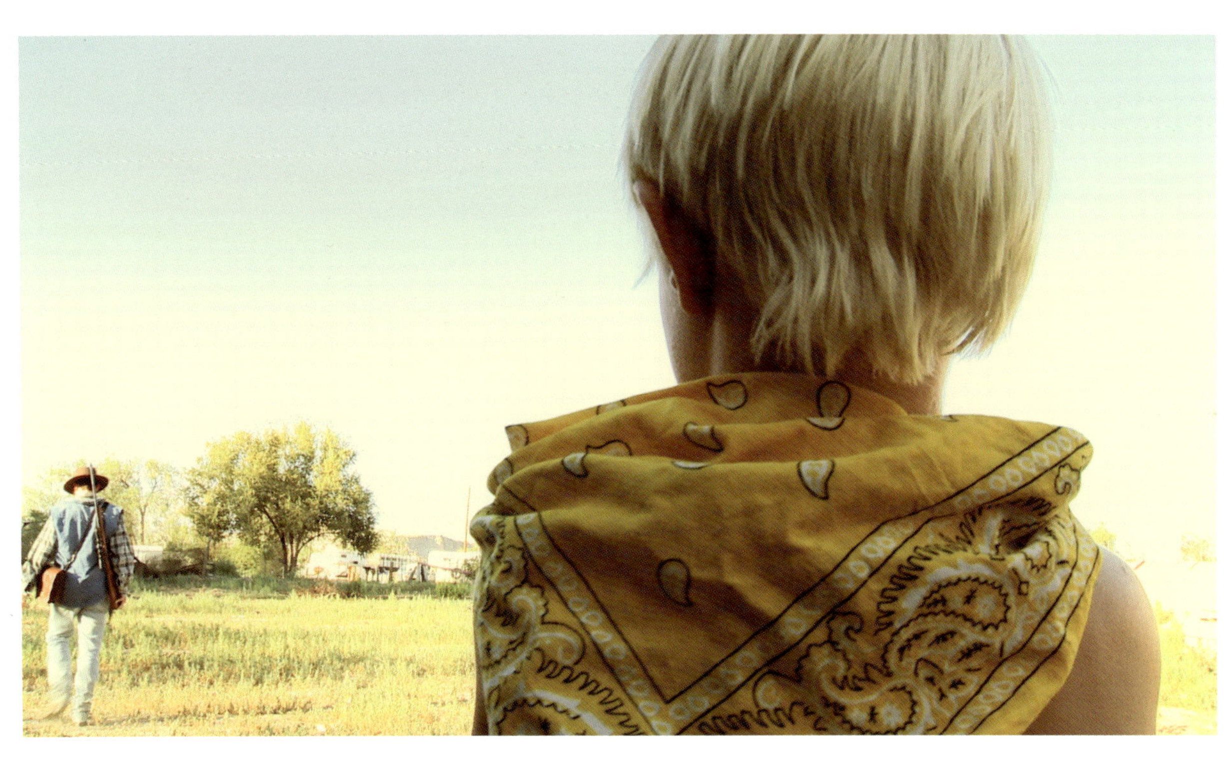

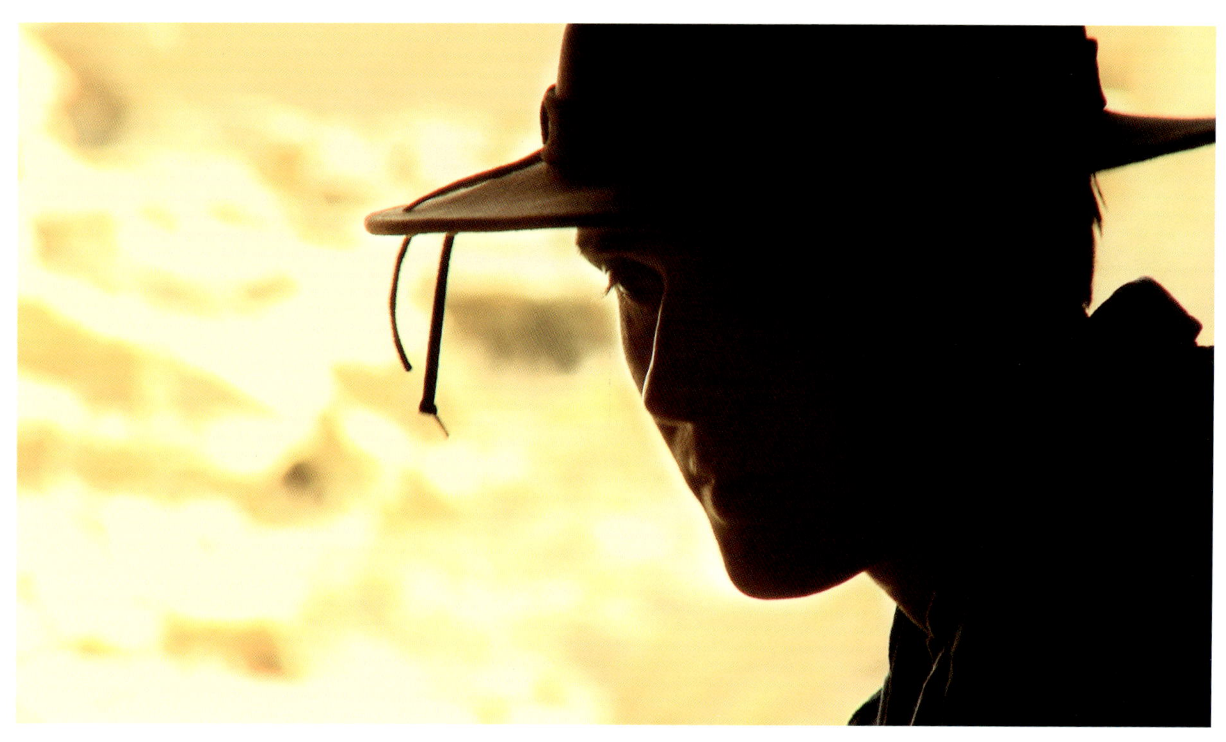

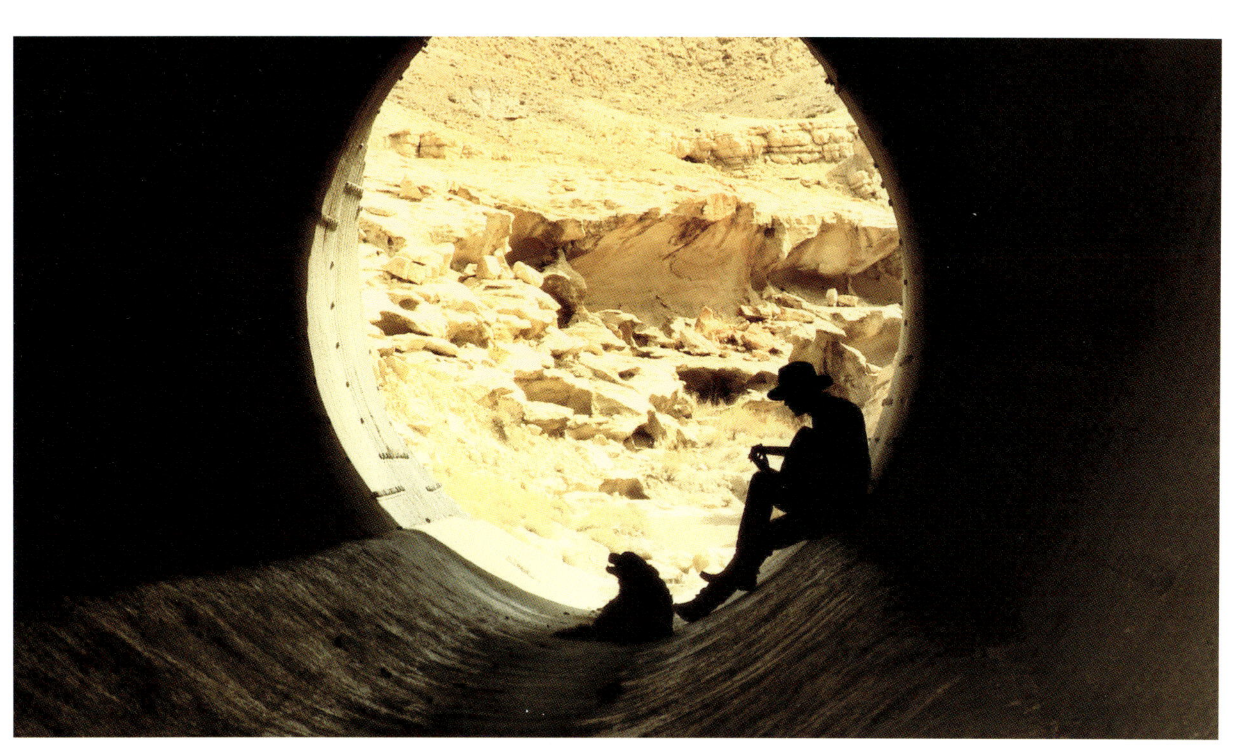

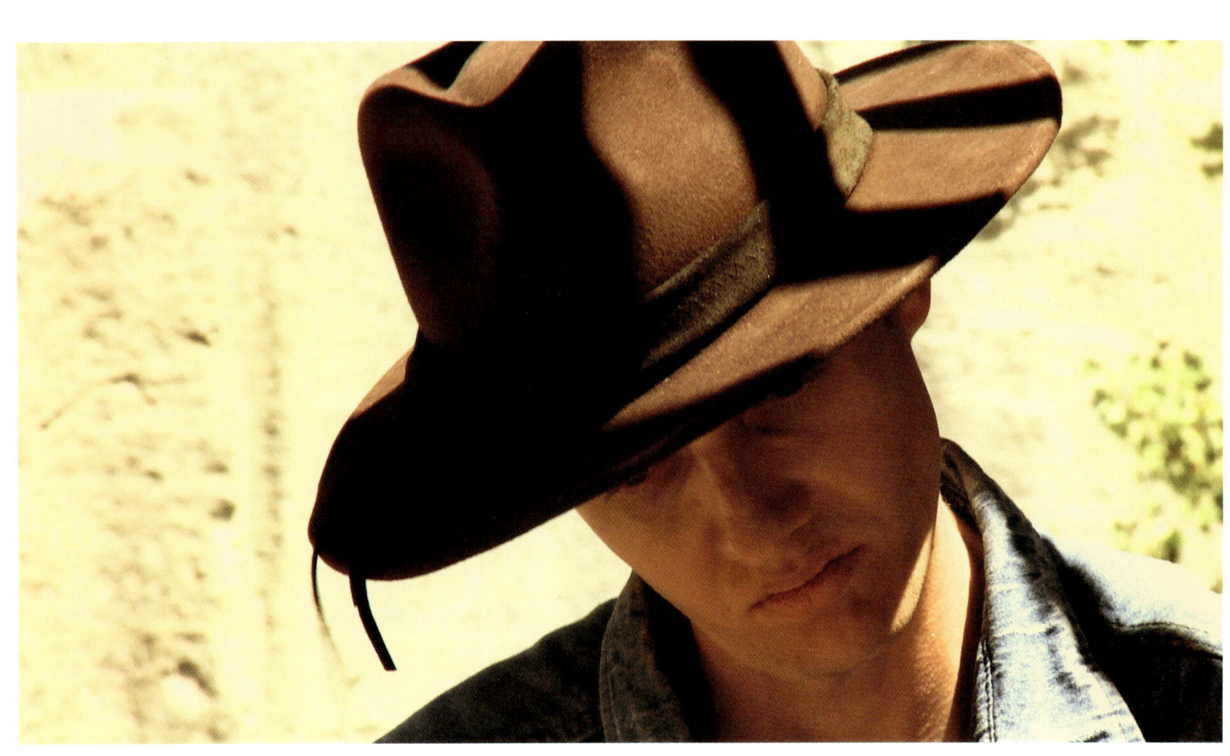

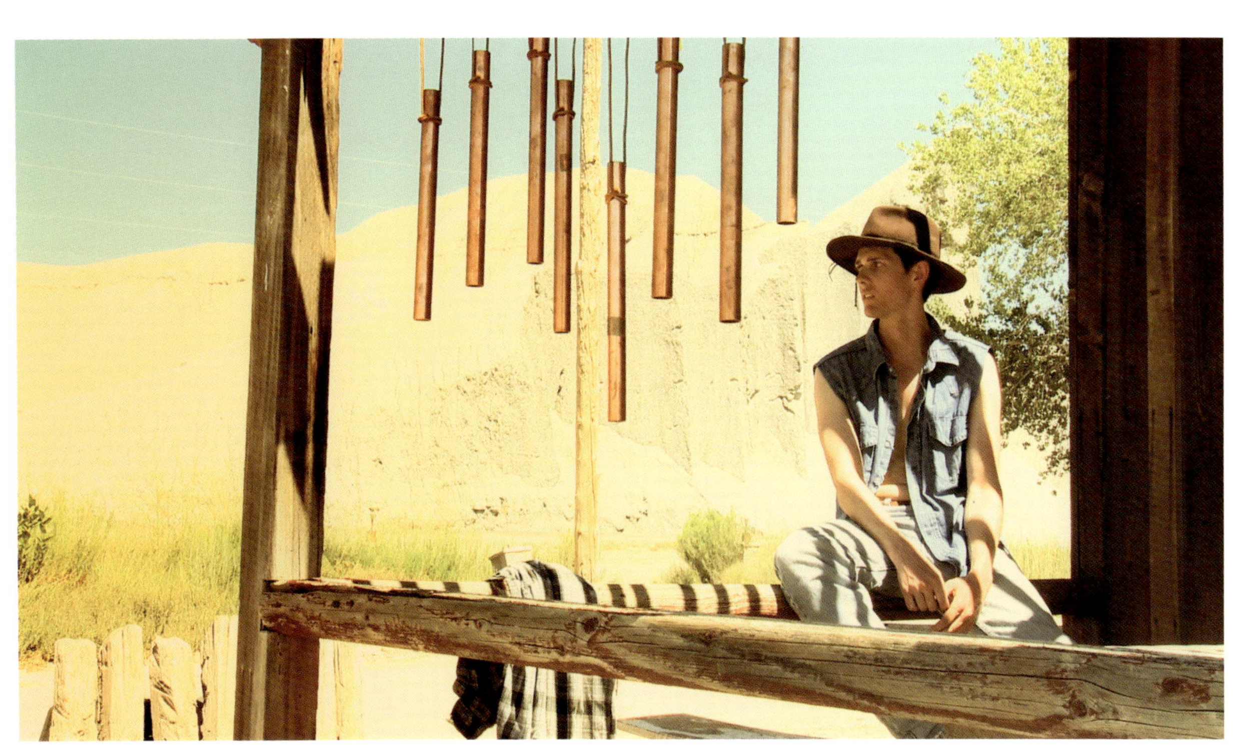

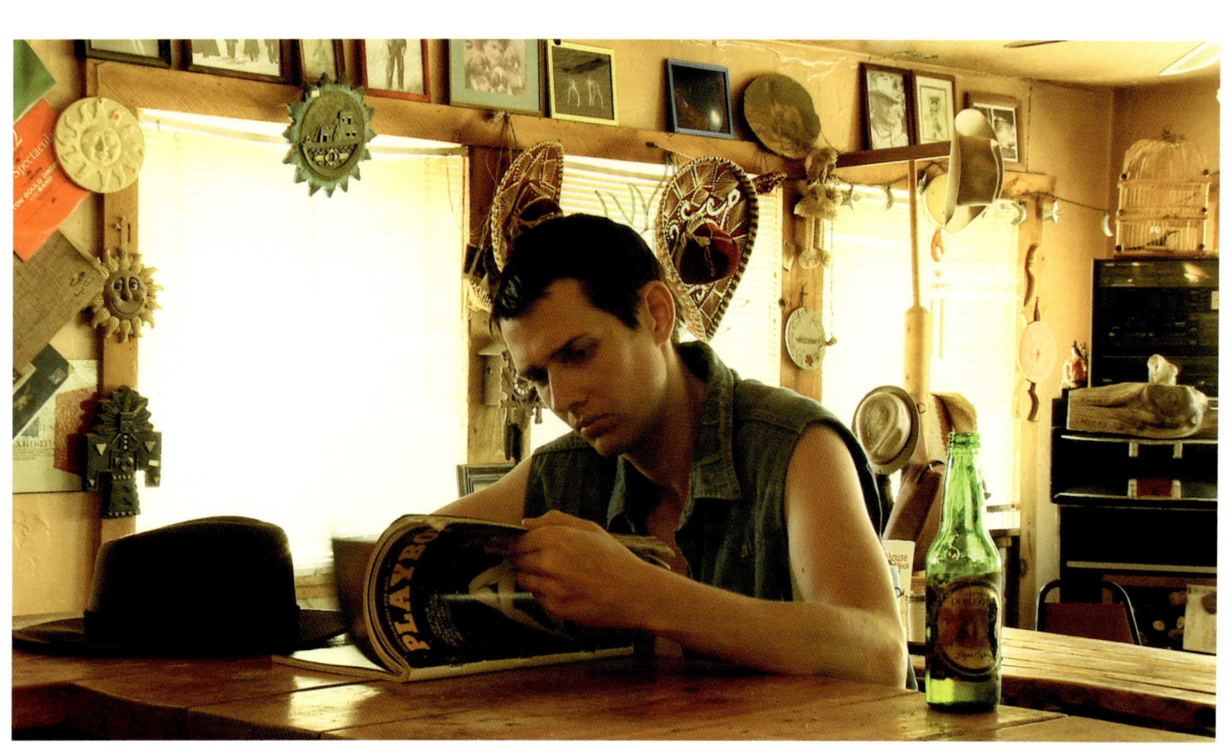

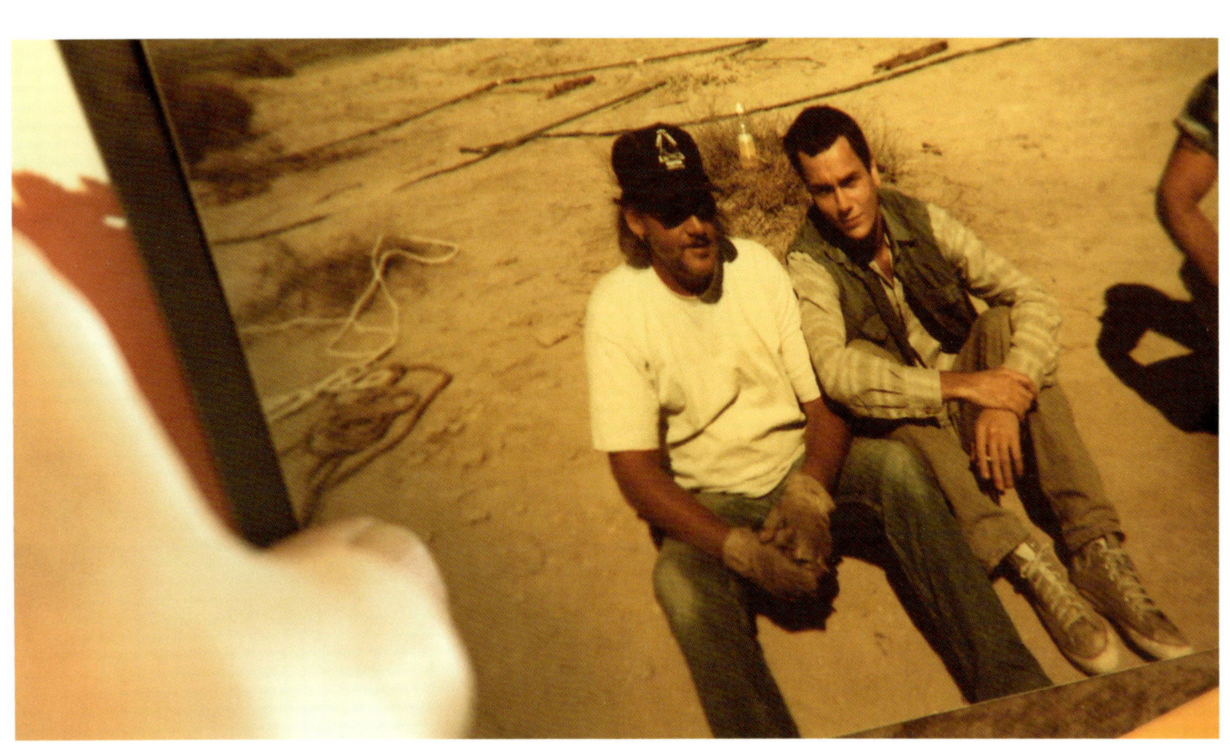

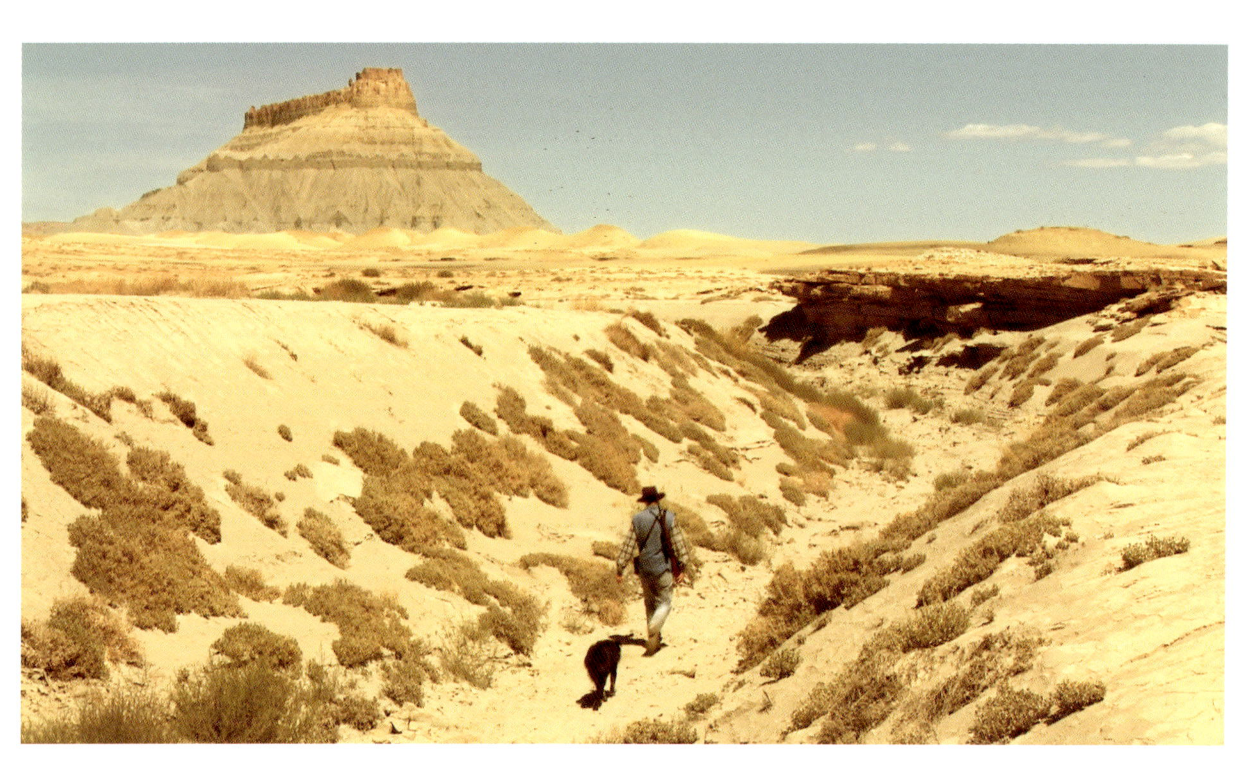

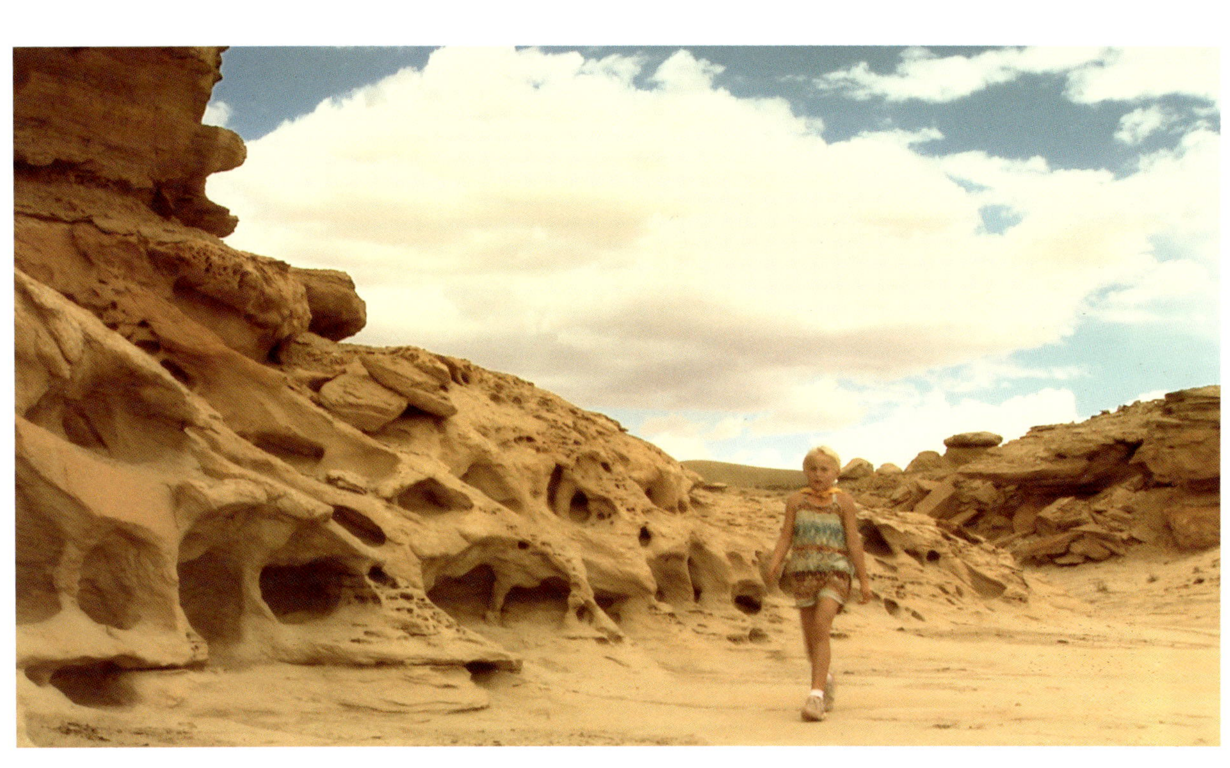

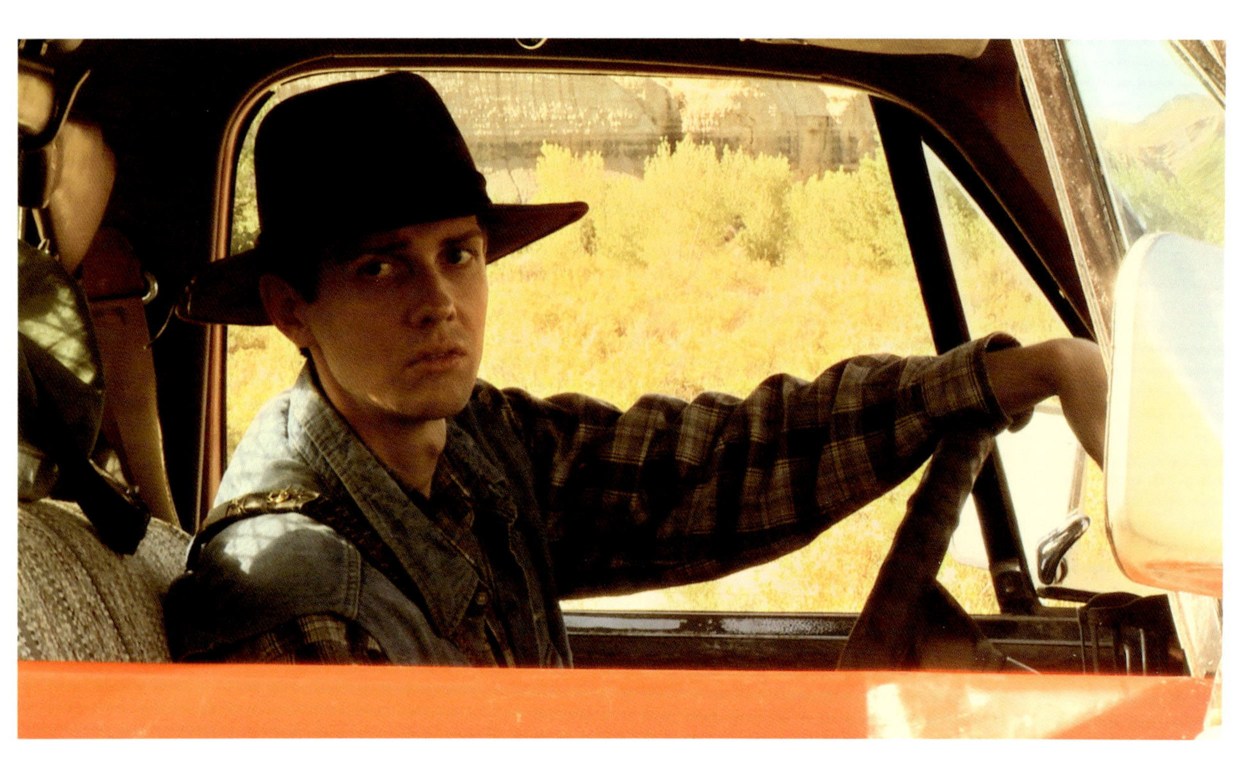

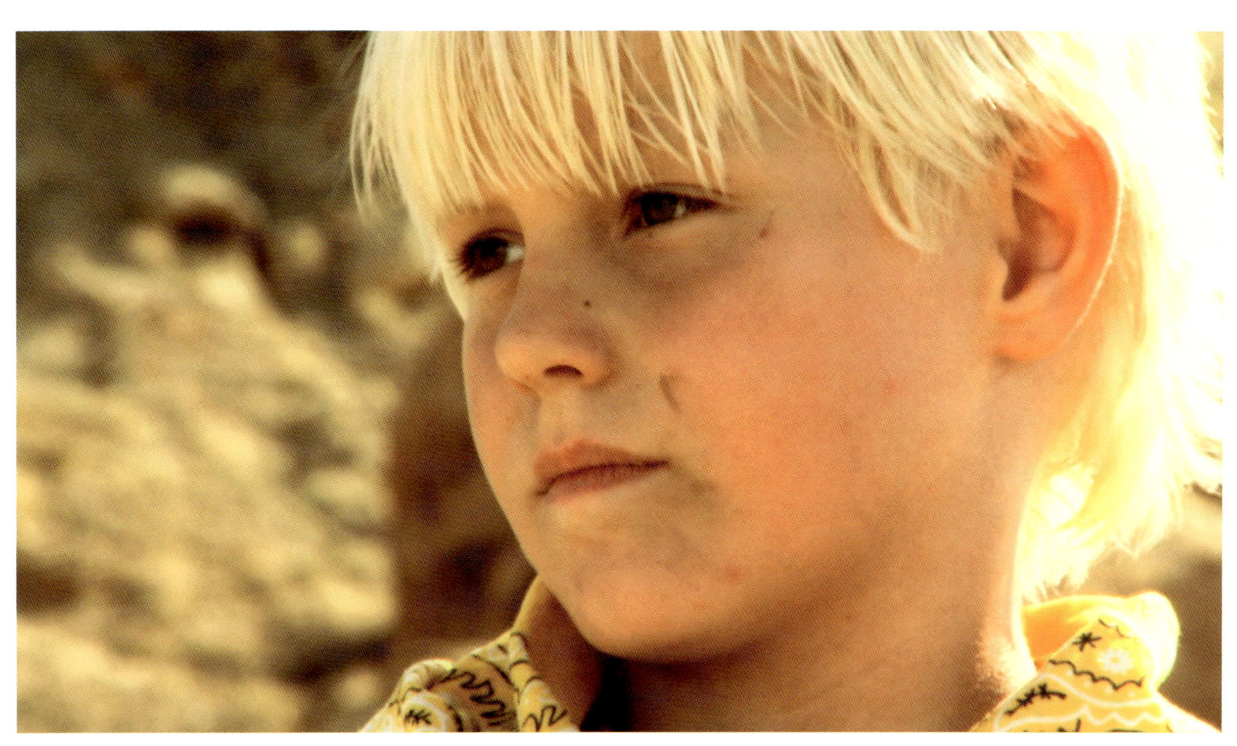

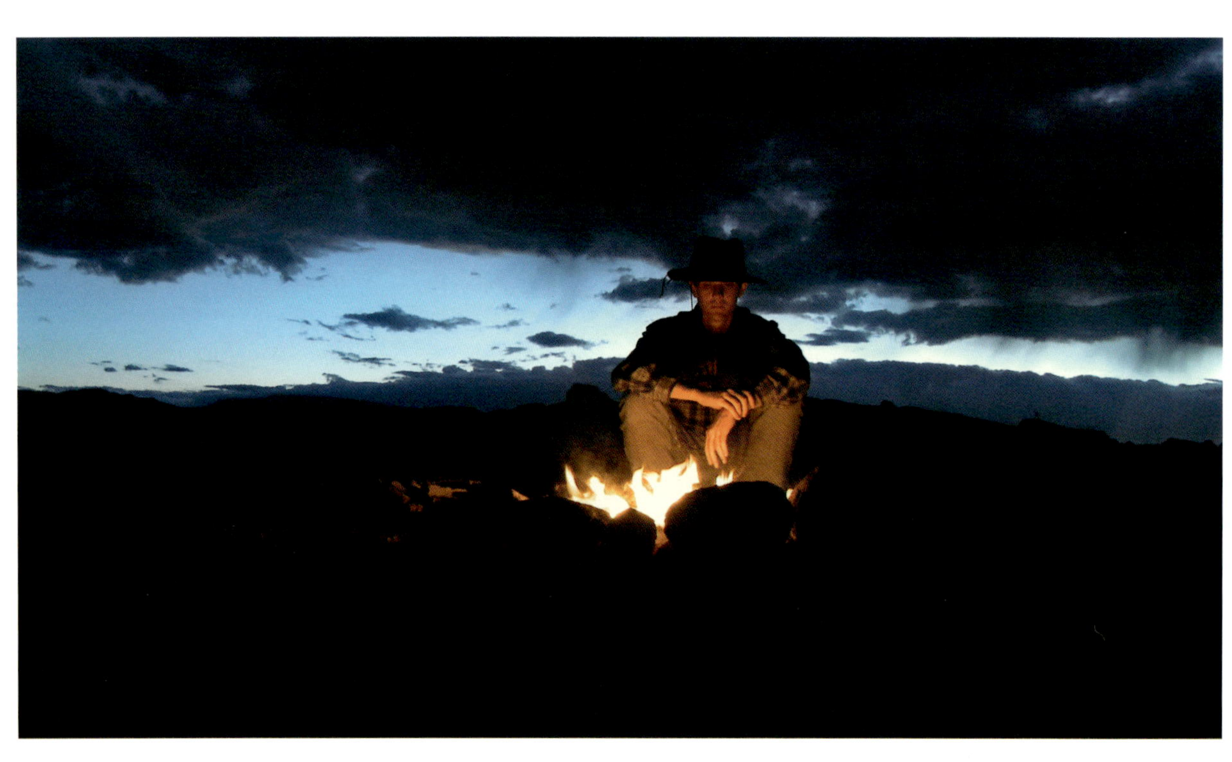

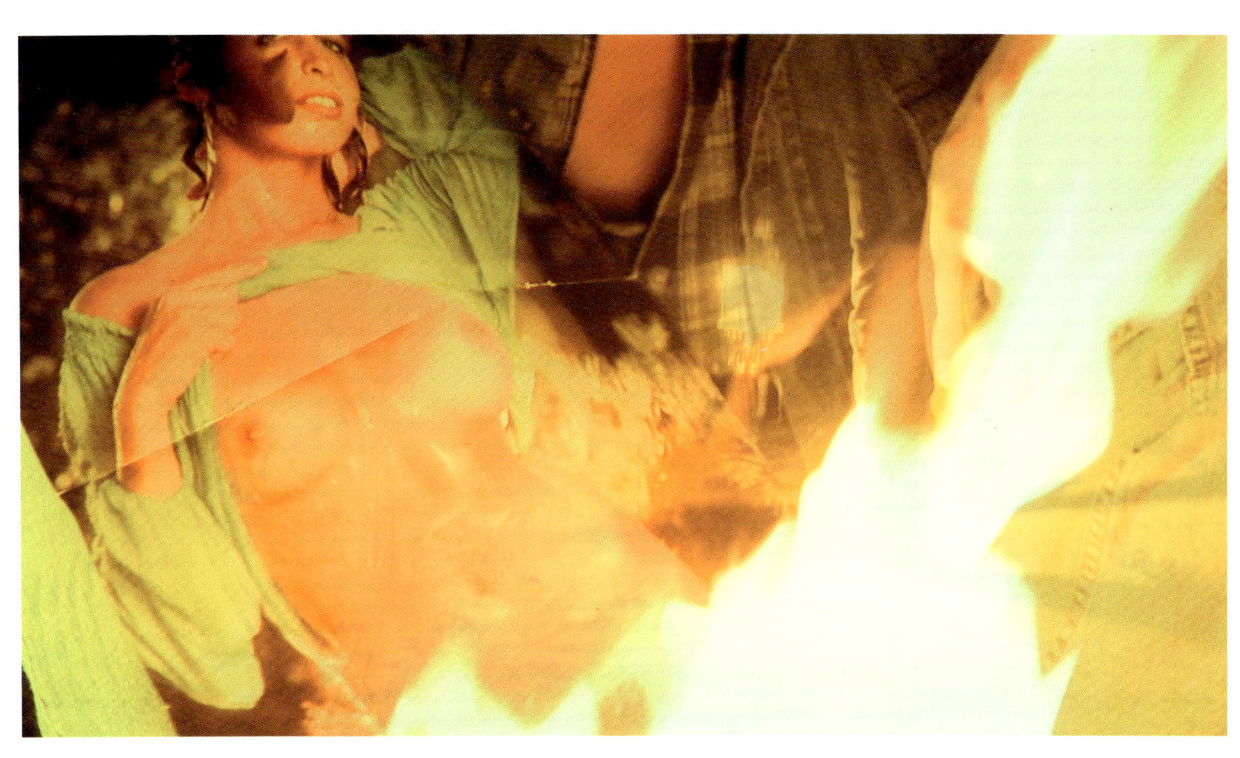

Ghosts

Slater Bradley and Ed Lachman
in conversation
with Heidi Zuckerman Jacobson

Heidi: Slater, I wanted to start off by asking you how you became aware of Ed and his work?

Slater: I actually heard about Ed when I was interning with Harmony Korine. I guess Ed was friends with Larry Clark, and they codirected *Ken Park* (2002), which turned out to be a—I guess that's another story. But I had heard about Ed through Harmony in 1997, and then, I don't know. Then I saw the YouTube clips where he talks about River. I think that was the next time I consciously realized that I was thinking about Ed in particular. When *Far from Heaven* (2002) came out, which Ed had worked on, I was really moved by that film.

Heidi: Ed, when Slater contacted you for the first time, were you aware of him and his work?

Ed: Actually not, and I took a long time because a lot of people contact me about doing something about River, and I was always kind of sensitive about that because the level of exploitation around his death. He was a very extraordinary person and became a friend. Slater sent me a lot of his work, to get interest in his project. Eventually I got around to looking at it, and I thought there was something in what he wanted to create through his ideas and images.

So then we talked about it. In an interview that Slater saw,
I talked about this last image that I photographed of River
in which he performed a long soliloquy in this cave that
we built in LA. We had just come back from Utah after
shooting there for eight weeks. There was already a lot of
tension because of the relationship between Judy Davis and
the director, George Sluizer, and River felt in between
because he always wanted to be the mediator. We actually
had to shut down for part of the first day of shooting in LA
because the cave wasn't fire retardant for safety regulations.
So we had to wait around half a day for the fire department
to retard this papier-mâché cave that made us all a little sick.
It was quite large, like eight feet around in diameter. There
were candles encompassing the cave like an altar.

River did this soliloquy, and it was apocalyptic, what he was
saying. He's prophesying his love for Judy Davis's character
and talking about the end of the world because the film
dealt with a lot of the issues that River was close to: the
environment, animal rights, and how Native Americans and
other minorities are abused in our culture.

Slater: Nuclear tensions as well.

Ed: So we did, I think, about four takes, and during the last take,
when I heard "cut," I turned the camera off. But my assistant
inadvertently turned the camera back on, thinking he was
turning it off. The film lights were dimmed down overhead;
they were lighting the tunnel but giving the illusion that it
was being lit by all the candles mounted in the cave. Then
River just became this perfect silhouette, like a cardboard
cutout. He just stood there.

The filming took place on a Saturday night, but we all
saw this on Monday morning, because we still had film
dailies back then. Just before this last take was screened, I
remembered that the camera hadn't turned off after cut. So
we were all in the screening room watching the last take and
heard the director say "cut." But the camera was still rolling;

we saw the lights go down, and then we saw River as a silhouette, like a ghost.

Then the most eerie part of it was when he walked up to the camera and his body covered the lens. The screen just went black. When we saw that, it was like the most eerie, out-of-body experience, almost prophetic. It just left everybody in shock and sadness.

So I discussed this for the BBC. I didn't know it, but they did a reenactment, and a poor one. I guess River—sorry, I always call Slater River—Slater saw that interview and that's the reason he contacted me.

Slater: I think the doppelganger (Ben Brock) actually saw it. I was always trying to find a way to make a piece about River because he was one of my formative influences. But it was very difficult for me to wrap my head around an idea. When I saw that clip, with that sort of liminal space, with the camera cutting off and River almost fading out of his own self during that 15 seconds, I felt that we could do a project about that moment. Yeah, so we began the journey there and here we are now.

Ed: In truth, we were realizing it was probably too expensive to recreate that set.

Slater: We were going to do it, but then we ran into the recession, and everything kind of turned over on its heels, so we decided to…

Ed: I thought it would be great to revisit that landscape because that landscape meant so much to the film and to me. I actually ended up buying land out there.

Slater: We decided to do a more off-the-cuff kind of piece, which is the kind of mode I've always worked in, where you just kind of have an idea and you just kind of go there and…

Ed: And create our own narrative.

Slater: Ed was like, "Let's let the landscape speak to us," and we kind of did.

Ed: It was a way of channeling River's spirit through the lost images.

Heidi: Let's talk about that for a second. You filmed *Shadow* (2010) in the same landscape, the same bar, and the same location, but how many years later?

Slater: They filmed in 1993. We shot the film in 2009, and then we edited it and showed it in 2010. So we literally shot it sixteen years later and showed it seventeen.

Heidi: Did you feel River's presence as part of the project?

Ed: Well, we found things like those images in the bar. That was a bar we always went to. It was the only bar in the area near Factory Butte, where we shot it, and the owners had been friends of River and the crew. They found a shoe box with photos in it while we were there. It was kind of like his ghost finding the real image of himself.

Slater: Over the course of the project, there were a lot of coincidences with holidays and anniversaries. To get our feet wet working together, we shot in April on Good Friday and Easter of 2009; we shot the façade of the Viper Room with two different Super 8 cameras and Ed's panoramic 6 x 17 cm camera. I don't think we intentionally picked Easter weekend to work together, but it happened that way. So by chance, from the outset, the project began as a kind of resurrection.

The first day that we arrived in Utah, I believe it was a Sunday, was River's birthday. That day the doppelganger had a call time of 6:00 in the morning and I went to his room. We were in this weird hotel at the edge of… where's that hotel, Ed? Do you remember?

Ed: Capitol Reef.

Slater: Yeah, the edge of Capitol Reef National Park. I went to find Ben, and Ben wasn't there. He was hiding in a dark corner down the hallway at the edge of this kind of deck that overlooks the desert because he had seen a ghost. Ben is not the kind of guy who has ever seen a ghost, as far as I'm aware, or has ever told me about it. The ghost, if I remember correctly, was kind of a midget tranny. I think it was a reference to this kachina doll thing: he said it was a skirted figure that jumped on the edge of his bed. He got up and threw himself against the wall while this figure was dancing on the edge of the bed.

He was completely freaked out. I remember we were going to shoot the first day—it was 100 degrees, 105 degrees, or whatever—and he's like, "You won't believe this." So he was telling everybody in the car about it, and then I remembered it was August 23rd and said "Oh, I think this is River's birthday." River died on Halloween. When Ed found these recent Polaroids from the cave, he called me on July 4th. So there's been this series of anniversaries that unfolded throughout the project and feel very connected.

Heidi: Serendipity plays a key role in your work. I wonder, because it's been going on such a long time, how much of that do you think is part of a larger, universal, abstract connection?

And at what point do you think you became hyperaware of these circumstances? Do you still think it's serendipity, or do you think that you have an awareness that allows you to utilize them to the benefit of your work?

Slater:

I always feel like when they happen I'm on the right path, and it's sort of a guiding mechanism. Because there is a certain—let's maybe not call it apprehension, but when I start these projects, I always try and look at them from every angle. Sometimes I think it's maybe pretentious, assuming, or just weird to want to make something about a tragic hero and bring them back to life in some way. I think every time that I get one of these coincidences, it really sort of reassures me that it's okay to do it. I've always been into numbers, I was always really into baseball statistics, and I just have a clarity with dates. I'm able to remember dates really well. It's just basically about feeling that it's okay—that whatever spirit I'm channeling when I have these experiences syncs up with the universe and it's okay.

Heidi:

That's interesting.

Ed:

Yeah, for me, the idea of the project, which maybe was different for Slater—and that's interesting too—is that when one creates an illusion in reality, which is really what film is, what happens if reality is seen as an illusion? So I was kind of revisiting the illusion to find a new reality. In a weird way, I was a doppelganger of myself, because he was asking me to recreate an image on the same set, on the same landscape as I had before because we were trying to mimic the images with his ghost or his doppelganger, Slater's doppelganger, through the lens where I was seventeen years ago. So in a weird way I became a ghost of the same image.

Heidi:

And how did that feel?

Ed: Well, that's why I was interested in the project. I was
           interested how I could reclaim an image that was lost. I've
           always been interested that people see film as reality in itself,
           but it's only an illusion. Just because we see images that
           represent an object, we don't have to get hung up thinking
           that reality is the object.

Slater: It's a slippage between fiction and reality that film activates.

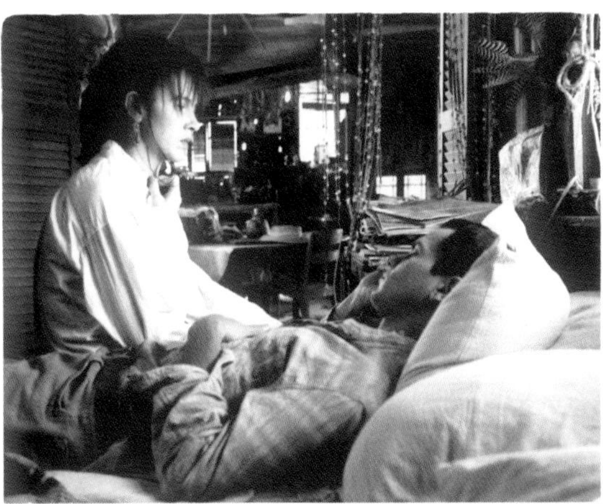 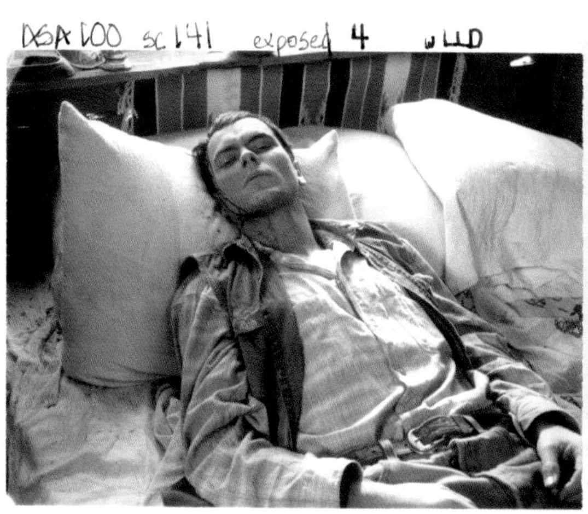

Ed Lachman, exposure-test black-and-white Polaroids taken on the set of *Dark Blood* (George Sluizer, 1993).

Ed: Film itself is the illusion. So this for me was about how you
           play with that, like creating the illusion of the illusion in the
           same reality.

Slater: Getting really meta there [laughs].

Ed: Sorry, sorry.

Heidi: So how do you feel about the finished product, Ed? How
           does it compare to what you thought it would be?

Ed:

What Slater was saying about filmmaking as a search for something, that's always what I felt films are anyway. All films are documents of something. Even a narrative becomes something different than what's written on a page. So if you're open to experience while filming, then you approach films in either narrative or documentary form as an uncharted journey.

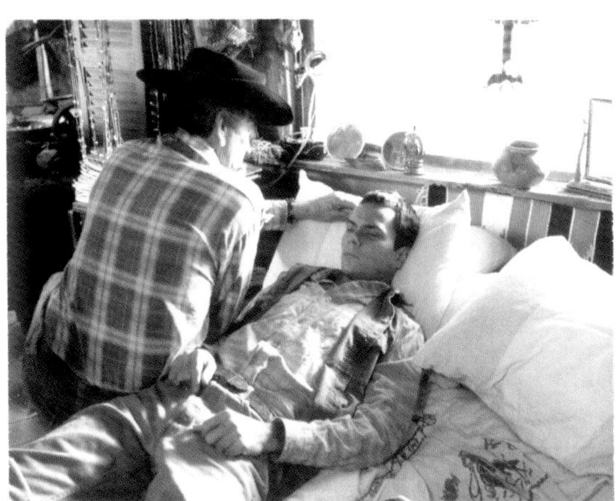

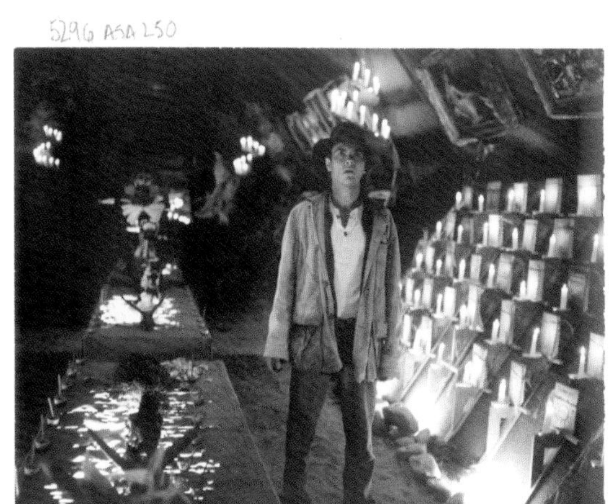

Slater:

I think the easiest way to answer that is to go back to the first time we were shooting the Viper Room. We went to Ed's storage locker in LA, and we looked through all these boxes of photos…

Ed:

Black-and-white Polaroids that I take on set for exposure checks.

Slater:

So we looked through all these boxes. Ed's meticulous in his labeling, but that doesn't necessarily mean you can find things when you want to. We were looking for these lost *Dark Blood* Polaroids, and we found *The Limey* (1999) Polaroids, *Erin Brockovich* (2000) Polaroids—we found this retrospective of Ed's work in his storage unit—but we didn't find any of the River Polaroids. Then three years later, Ed found them in New York because he was doing a renovation.

Ed: I just happened to look in a box that they never should have been in. There they were in there with other negatives. I don't know how they got there, but there were these four Polaroids. They were actually taken the last day we shot with him, hours before the last time River was with us.

Slater: Probably the last images taken of River. The "Look Up and Stay in Touch" autograph that he did on the wall behind the bar in Utah—that's the title of this show—could have been his last autograph. I think the project has a sense of archeology to it. You search for meaning, and then to be guided through this labyrinthine project—taking, I think, over four years—and to find at the very end, right before we make this catalogue, to find these priceless images that communicate…

Ed: Well, they were the images that we were looking for in the beginning.

Slater: Right, and to find them at the end, it feels like a release of River's spirit, that there is this final "Here it is. It's okay." I don't know. It feels completely like a full-circle type of moment, and I think it's a really beautiful moment.

Ed: Like a puzzle that comes together.

Heidi: Do you think you can look up and stay in touch?

Slater: Yes!

Ed: Yes, but you have to want to.

Heidi: It's a nice thought though, right? Slater, as you've gone through the doppelganger series, a lot of the doppelgangers—not just Ben, your doppelganger, but let's call them parallel doppelgangers—have died. Have you thought about what that means for you?

Slater: I think the larger issue is, as human beings, how do we cope with loss? If you're so in love with something, or if something resonates in such a beautiful way with you that it creates this formation of your identity, and then it's suddenly ruptured—that relationship between the icon and fan—how do you cope with that? There doesn't seem to be a real coping mechanism in society other than street-side, JKF Jr.–style, fan-made letters and vigils. My art is interested in that space. How does one keep in touch? How does one keep the dialogue happening when the physical body dies? I guess when you fall in love with an icon and the energy that surrounds it, you're channeling a spirit; it's a spiritual connection. It's like delving into religion and all of those kinds of things.

Heidi: Are you a fan or is it more than that? Does the connection run deeper?

Slater: "Fandom" is kind of a dirty word. I don't necessarily like to ever hear my work described as an exercise in fandom or as a fandom ritual. I definitely think it runs much deeper. I think what's interesting about right now is that the relationship between icon and fan has completely collapsed. That's happened over the last ten years, which may be one of the reasons why this doppelganger project has resonated: because it's actually following the collapse of that space through technological advancements and obsolescence, as digital takes over analog. Now, whatever Kanye West is Twittering to the fans is a direct line of communication.

When I started this project, you could do things about Michael Jackson or Kurt Cobain on a fan network, but you never thought that the icon would actually see it or that it would get back to them. I wouldn't say it was masturbatory, but it was a self-indulgent type of act. But now there's a sense that this self-indulgent act actually goes back to the creator, which is very interesting. The dialogue is really rich in that way.

Heidi: These elements are quite intriguing because you create these self-portraits in a way that is absent your presence. That's one reason why *Dead Ringer* (2011) is so different. You've had someone else as a stand-in for yourself in these doppelganger works, and the doppelganger usually does some pretty great stuff, whether it's moonwalking or being by themselves in the Museum of Natural History. But here, for the first time, you actually come forth from... well, you break the screen, really, with your presence. In theory, some of your fans, to use that word again, may or may not know that's actually you, or which one is you. That's a clever mastery of your own image, which is something that the people who you are following and capturing and memorializing have succeeded in as well. And that's one definition of celebrity: selecting which "you," which persona, which presence to offer to those who need you.

Ed: It's also a way of him confronting his doppelganger, where the reality confronts the illusion.

Heidi: Absolutely.

Slater: I think one of the great conceptual ideas about the doppelganger is that, at some point, you know you have to confront this other and kill them, or be killed. Right before my doppelganger appeared, I was reading the annotated version of Nabokov's *Lolita* (1955). I can't remember it exactly, but there's a line at the end where Humbert Humbert kills his doppelganger, Clare Quilty—actually you should read this, it's really amazing—"Us rolled into we. We rolled into us."[1] There is this collapsing of elements through death… the end of the hunt… a collision course. At a certain point it's very taxing to always rely on somebody else to embody you, so I'm happy that the project has come to a point.

I also must say, Ed was very instrumental in this when we shot that scene. You have to imagine that you're in a desert next to Factory Butte, which can be seen from outer space. There's nothing else around, cell phones don't work, cars break down. It felt very isolated. It was about 2:00 in the afternoon, probably about 105 degrees, and we had done fourteen takes. Ben is almost psychopathic about this stuff, because he memorized the original scene from *Dark Blood* on YouTube. It's one of, I think, two clips that George Sluizer released (and that were shown on a Dutch TV documentary) where the actual footage of River was used. Ben memorized all the movements exactly. So it's Ben's big moment out there in the desert, and the guy, he won't let the moment end! We've done fourteen takes, and I'm sitting there trying to play… Ed what was the guy's name? The actor Jonathan Pryce, right?

Ed: Yeah, Jonathan Pryce. River's character had the big confrontation with him. We were recreating the scene. There was a dolly shot over the fellow, so you actually don't see him. So I thought, this is the time: let River go in—I said River again—let Slater go in and confront his own image.

---

[1] The quote reads: "We rolled all over the floor, in each other's arms, like two huge helpless children. He was naked and goatish under his robe, and I felt suffocated as he rolled over me. I rolled over him. We rolled over me. They rolled over him. We rolled over us." Vladimir Nabokov, *Lolita* (1955; New York: Random House, 1989), 298–99.

Slater: Yeah, I kind of just jumped into the frame.

Ed: He just came out of the blue. Basically it was the heat, or whatever…

Slater: I think I was just fed up with take after take after take. I mean this was day four or five, we were really burnt out, and I just kind of jumped into frame and pretended to kill him—extinguish him, I think, was the idea, extinguish him with a little bit of tenderness. I remember Ed said, "Wow, the shadow was cartoony and cool. You should do another take." There was this weird moment where I felt like I'd been pushed in. It was only because I trusted the experience Ed has with cinema that I would allow myself to take that sort of risk. I'm very self-conscious.

So we did a few more takes and called it a day after the twentieth take. Months later, we got back to the editing room and literally, I kid you not, it was the kind of thing where we said, "Oh, let's look at one of these takes where I jump in," and then "Okay, let's compare it to two other takes." So we juxtaposed the three best takes together on one screen. We didn't change anything. They all just worked perfectly. It was like watching a slot machine hit a jackpot.

Ed: It was strange. Maybe it was the heat, but my camera movement became the same on each take. In other words, I was recreating the same image, like a facsimile.

Heidi: Or a doppelganger.

Ed: Yeah, the image became its own doppelganger, which was really weird.

Slater: But is it was like an exploded version, a psychedelic version of it.

Heidi: That's the definition of a doppelganger, right? It's something you can't control?

Ed: It's a ghost double or counterpart of a living person.

Slater: Like an apparition that haunts you.

Ed: Or something that takes over.

Slater: Or portends your own death.

Ed: A doppelganger can be something that takes over an image.

Slater: The whole project started when I was twenty-three in 1998. I'd just come to New York from art school. I didn't really know anybody and I was just starting out. To hear that there's this other guy who looks like you, who people mistake you for, is a really depressing idea. It was like, "Oh, you've come to New York to make it, fresh out of UCLA, and then there's this guy who is already you and now you're kind of useless." So I thought that it was a great moment to be like, "Okay, well, if I can't make any impression as myself, I might as well just try and make an impression with my double as the vehicle."

Ed: But does the copy replace the original? That's a question for the doppelganger. What is the original? What's left of the original?

Slater: What we're seeing now is that the copy is just as important as the original, if not more so. That's how the original sustains its originality.

Ed: Well, I don't know if it's as important, but it's certainly the way society looks at things. Like in Japan, they built an Eiffel Tower and built it higher so the Japanese didn't have to go to France to see the real Eiffel Tower. They could have their own and it could be higher.

Slater: Right. So it's the replicant thing.

Heidi: Is there anything that we didn't talk about that you would like to address?

Ed: I related to the project personally through River and through this post-hippie consciousness of him, because I guess I came out of that period of the 1960s. He is a tragic figure and died with all this potential. He represented some type of spiritual ideal. He was killed by the very poisons he was in opposition to. He was an animal activist, a vegan, and an environmentalist, but in the end, he died by demons and poisons.

Slater: He was a prototype, really ahead of his time because now, twenty years later, all the things that he stood for are completely in vogue. But he's never really identified as a leader in the eco/green movement. He was a very beautiful actor and became an icon for that, but he was on the cusp of really becoming great. He was also a talented musician. In *Shadow*, the song Ben plays in a drainage ditch is "Height Down," a song River wrote with John Frusciante. River resonates a lot, but he's just not talked about or known now, which I think is really tragic. I think he's kind of lost for this generation.

Ed: He was kind of an egoless spirit. I remember one morning when I came out of my room and I didn't have my glasses on, and someone said, "Oh, can I help you with your cases?" I didn't know who it was, then I put on my glasses and it was River. I told him, "No, you don't have to help me with my cases. I can take them downstairs." But no, he wanted to help. He was always that way. He never put himself above anything or anybody.

Heidi: Is there a dedication in this project?

Slater: Well, I'd like to dedicate it to Matty Mascotte, my friend that died of intestinal cancer. The way Ed describes River I would describe Matty, as the most selfless person. He had cancer for five years and I never heard him complain once. He always wanted to cheer me on, and because he had an identical twin, he really understood the territory that I was working in and was fascinated by that. I never really had a friend like Matty, and I really miss him.

Ed: There's one other little footnote, which I don't even want to bring it up, but it's very strange. I worked on three films in which actors have died.

Heidi: During the film?

Ed: Well, during or soon after we wrapped. In *They All Laughed* (1981), Dorothy Stratten; River in *Dark Blood;* and Heath Ledger in *I'm Not There* (2007).

Heidi: You were working on that one too?

Ed: Yes, I was the Director of Photography on that.

Slater: There's one other thing that I'm glad I remembered— another sort of psychic moment. In 2009 I was working on a show at Team called *if we were immortal*, which was based on Joy Division paraphernalia. When I was twelve I discovered the myth of Ian Curtis, the singer for that band. The night he killed himself, he was watching Herzog's *Stroszek* (1977) on TV. I don't really know how people know that for sure, but apparently that's what he was doing. Interestingly enough, Peter Saville, who cofounded Factory Records and designed several Joy Division album covers, is consulting on this catalogue, so there's definitely a Joy Division wave through this project. So I was working on the show and on one of the classic images in the mythology of Joy Division, the dancing chicken…

Ed: Which is at the end of *Stroszek*.

Slater: The main character, Bruno S., is an immigrant who comes to America to follow the American dream. He doesn't succeed, has everything taken back by the bank, and kills himself. There's a parallel here to Ian Curtis, who killed himself on the eve of Joy Division's American tour. That was May 18, 1980, which is also the day that Mount Saint Helens erupted. In addition to making the painting of the dancing chicken, I was also working on a project about the fact that nobody had made a Joy Division Mount Saint Helens bootleg. So Bruno S. goes into a sort of amusement park in Wisconsin, right before he kills himself on a ski lift, and there are all these live animals playing instruments in coin-operated dioramas. The chicken is dancing on a hot plate and playing piano; it's very Herzogian, very weird, and very cryptic.

I remember one of the first times that we were meeting in my studio to talk about what we were going to do for *Shadow*. Ben says "Ed, tell us about working with Werner Herzog." And I was like, "What are you talking about? I didn't know that Ed worked with Herzog!" Ben said, "Well, he shot second camera for *Stroszek*."

Ed: Well, I shot the American part.

Slater: So I said "Ed, you shot the dancing chicken? Look at this painting!"

Ed: Yeah, I had just noticed the painting in your studio.

Slater: I showed him this painting of the dancing chicken, which is synonymous for me with evil and darkness—really, the most fucked-up energy you can muster—and I said, "You shot this? And he was like, "Yeah, I shot this." That was another moment where my head exploded. It was mythological perfection.

       I guess in some sort of way, as an artist, you've just got to kind of keep the myth going. You've got to add to the myth. I feel like this collaboration does that. It keeps these things in conversation and keeps them going. That was just an incredible coincidence, which really made me feel, again, that the whole project was worth doing and that everything was going to turn out okay in the end.

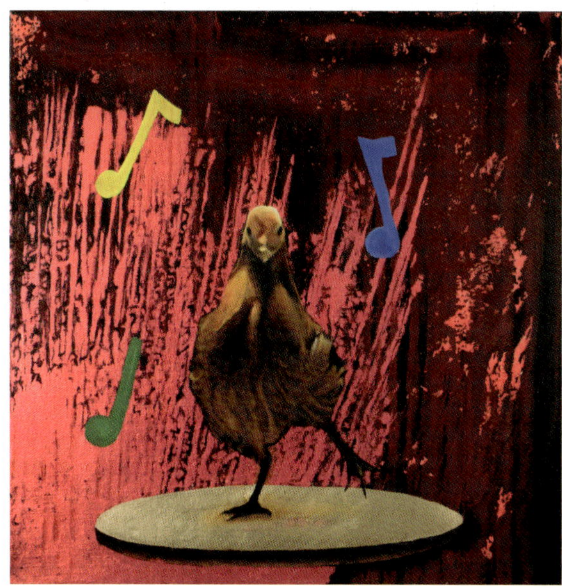

Slater Bradley, *Lachman's Legacy*, 2009.

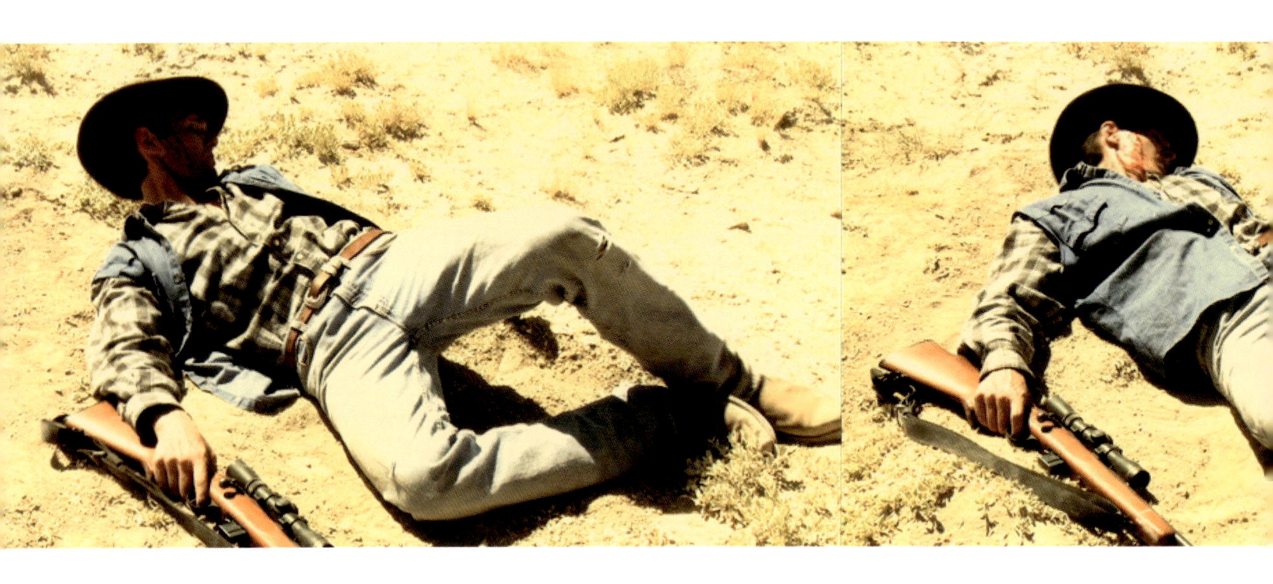

Dead Ringer

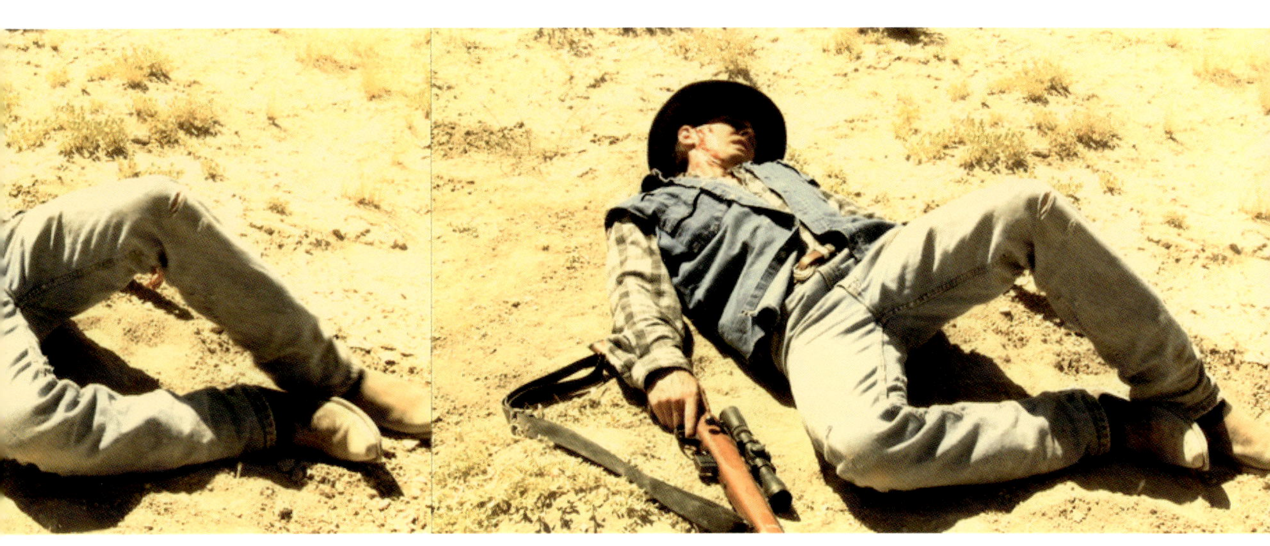

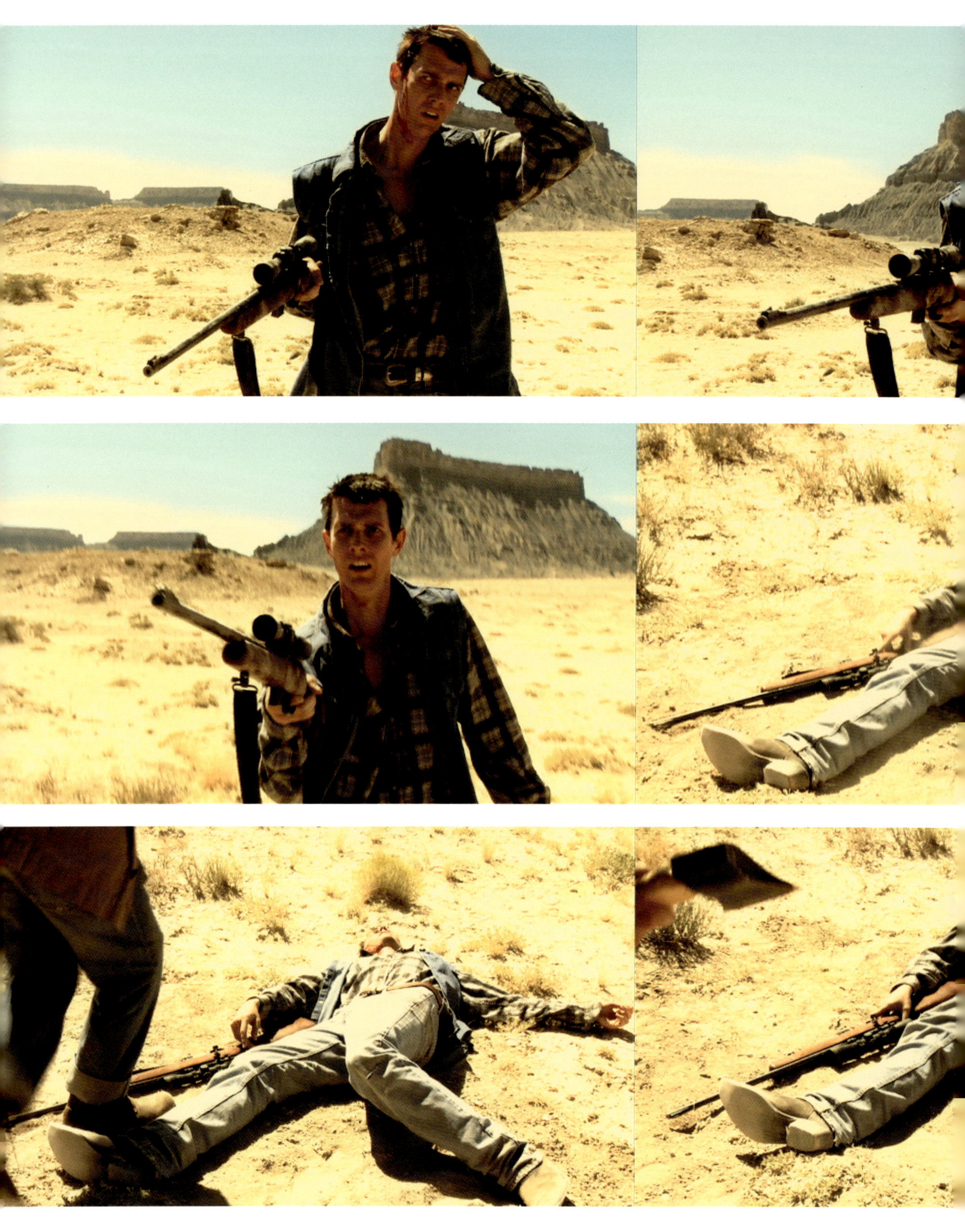

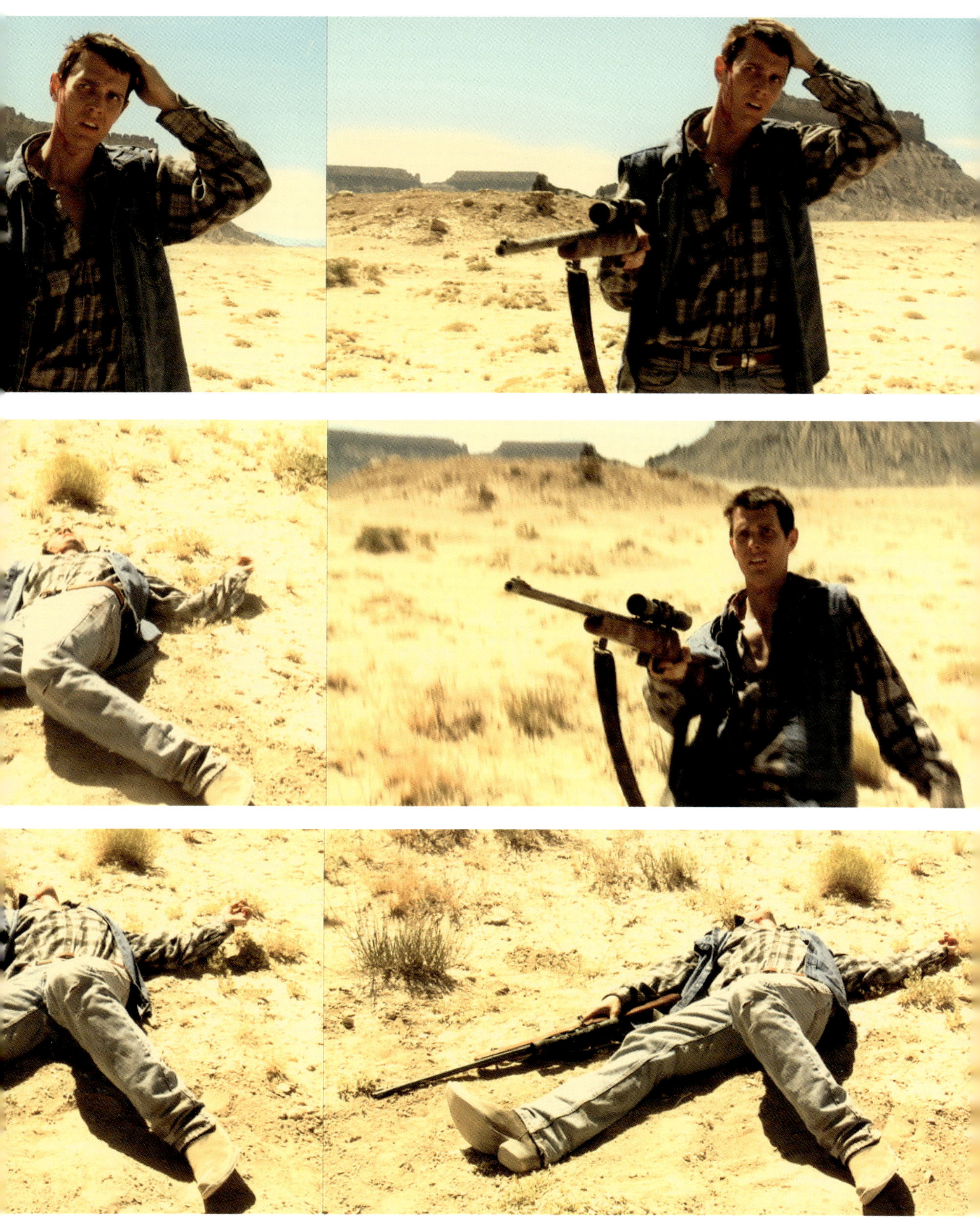

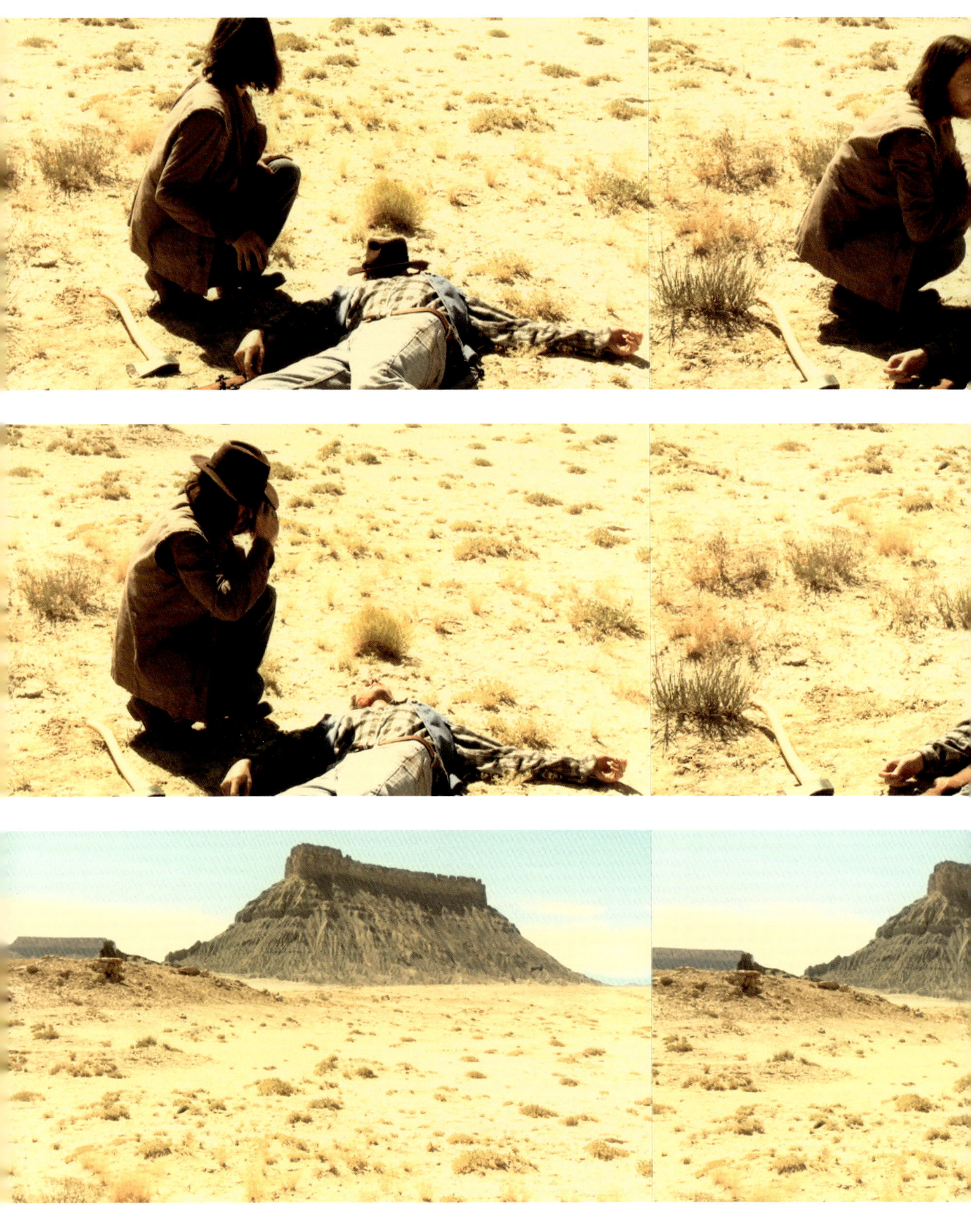

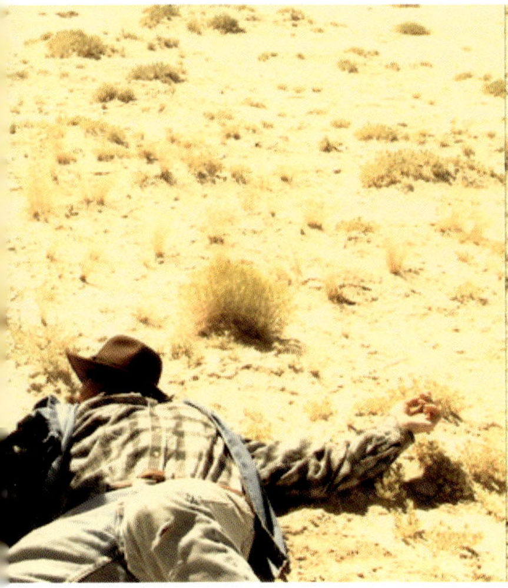

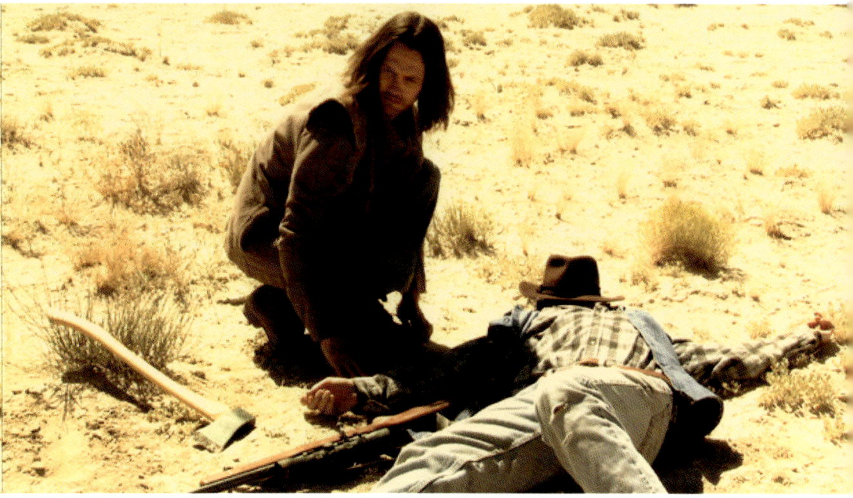

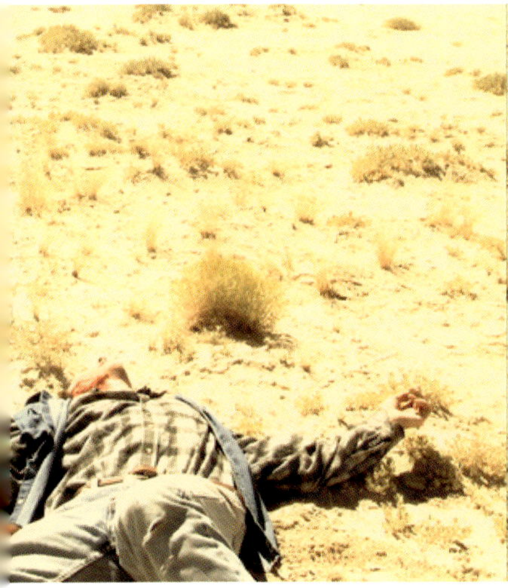

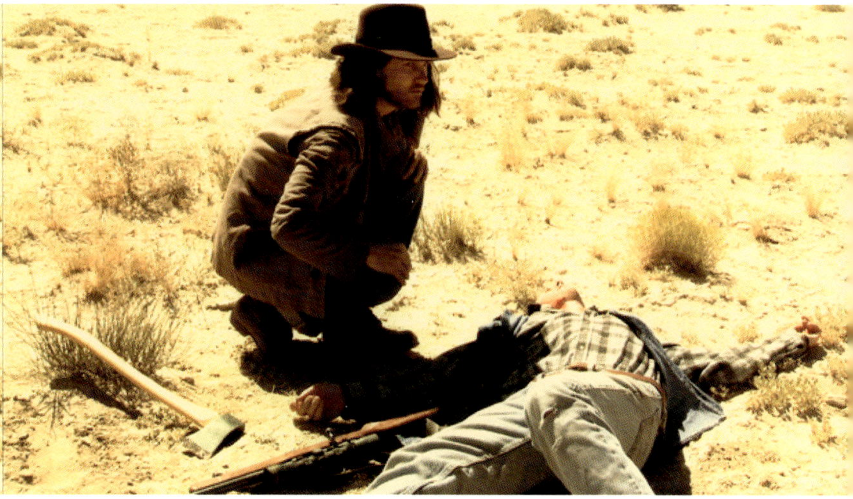

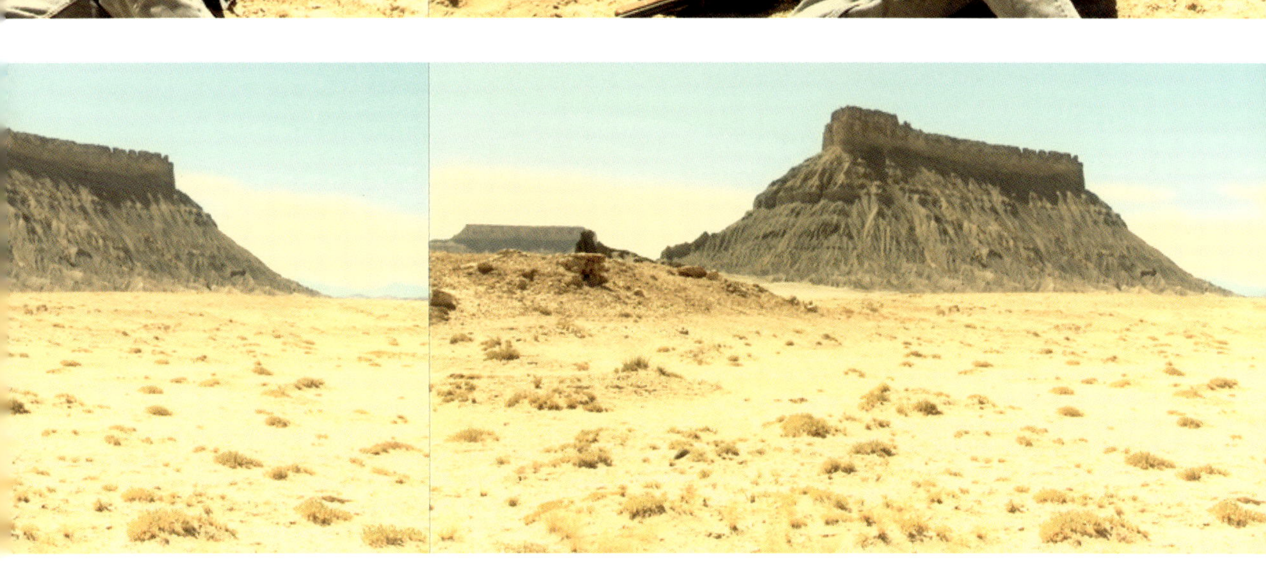

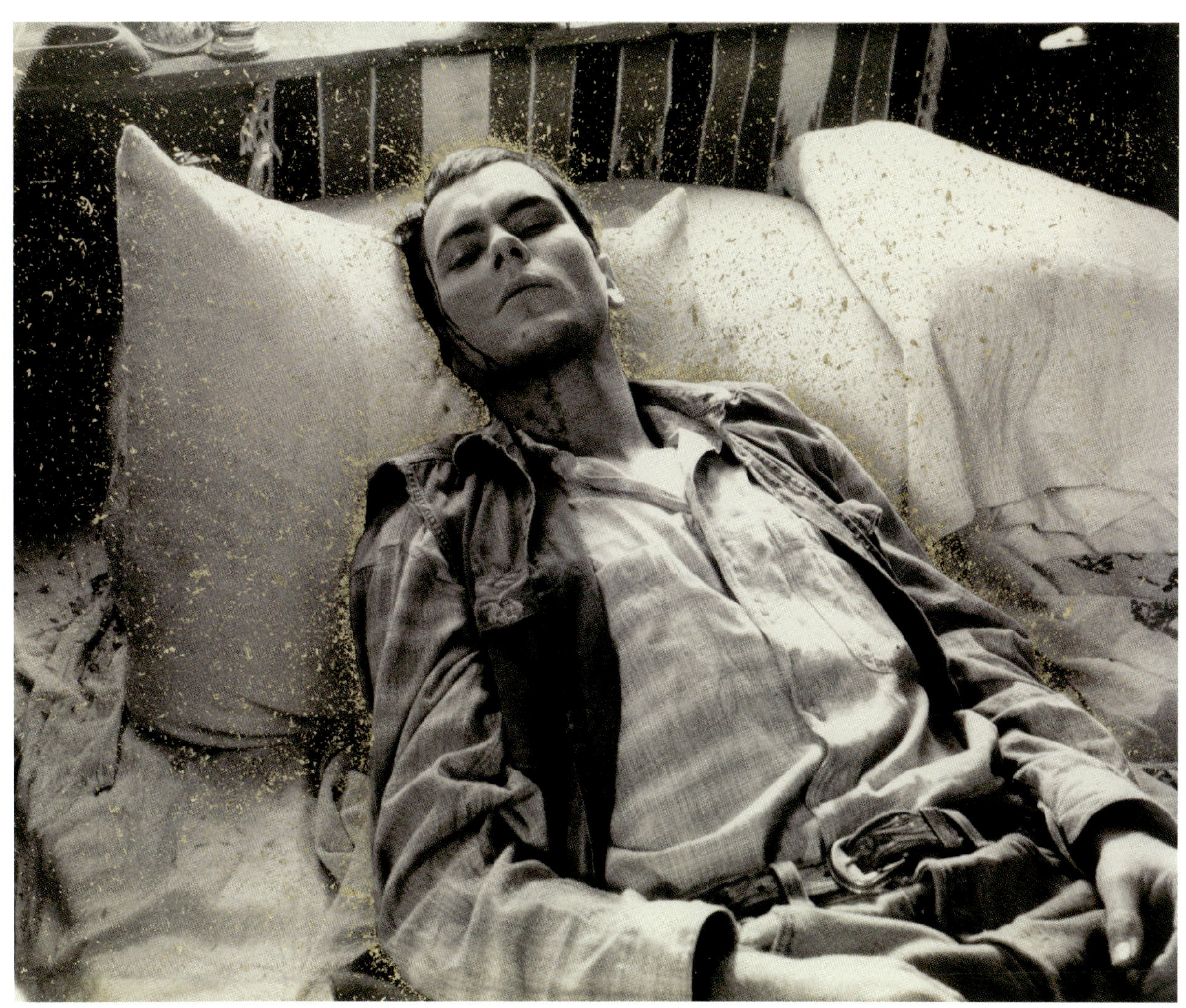

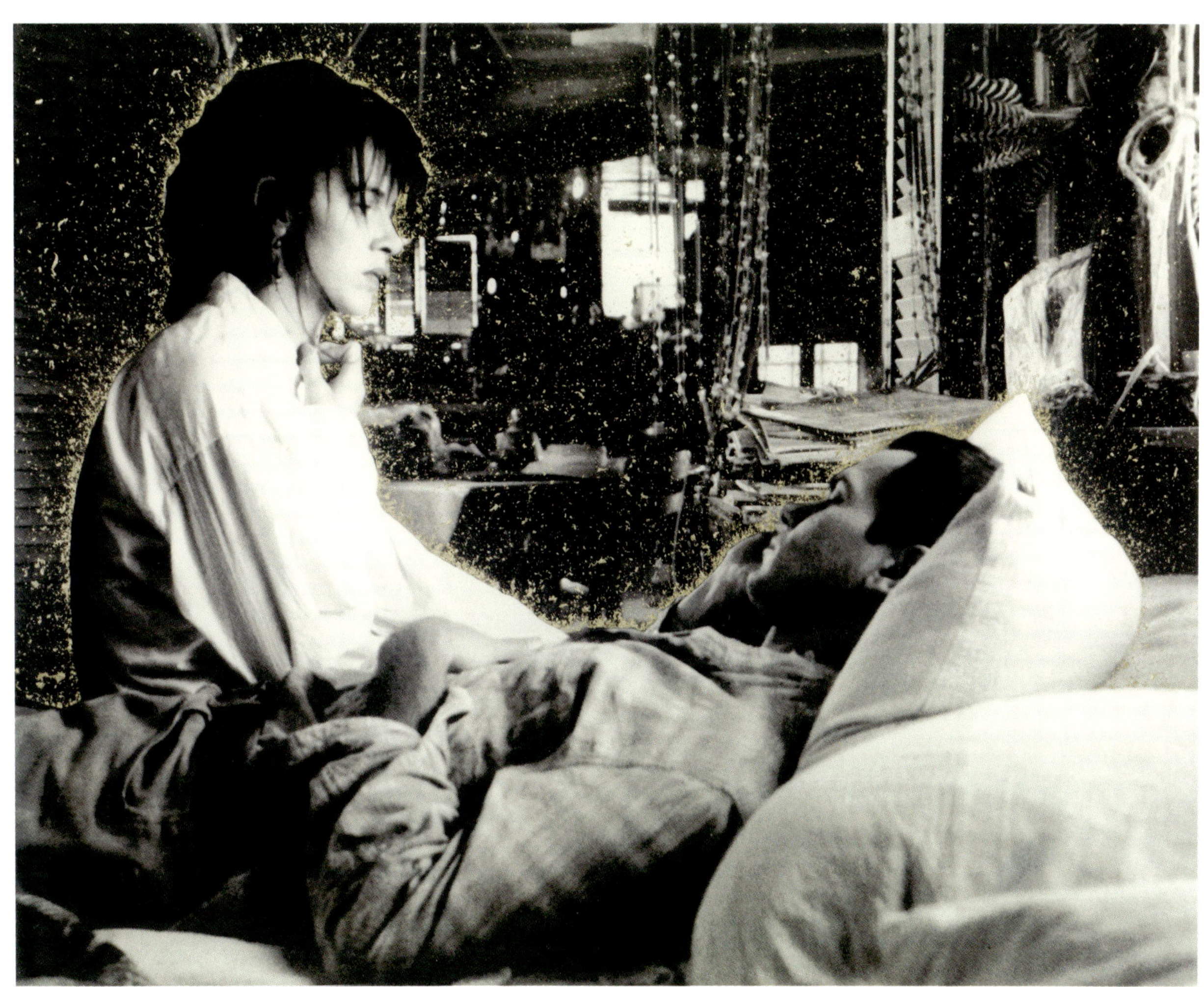

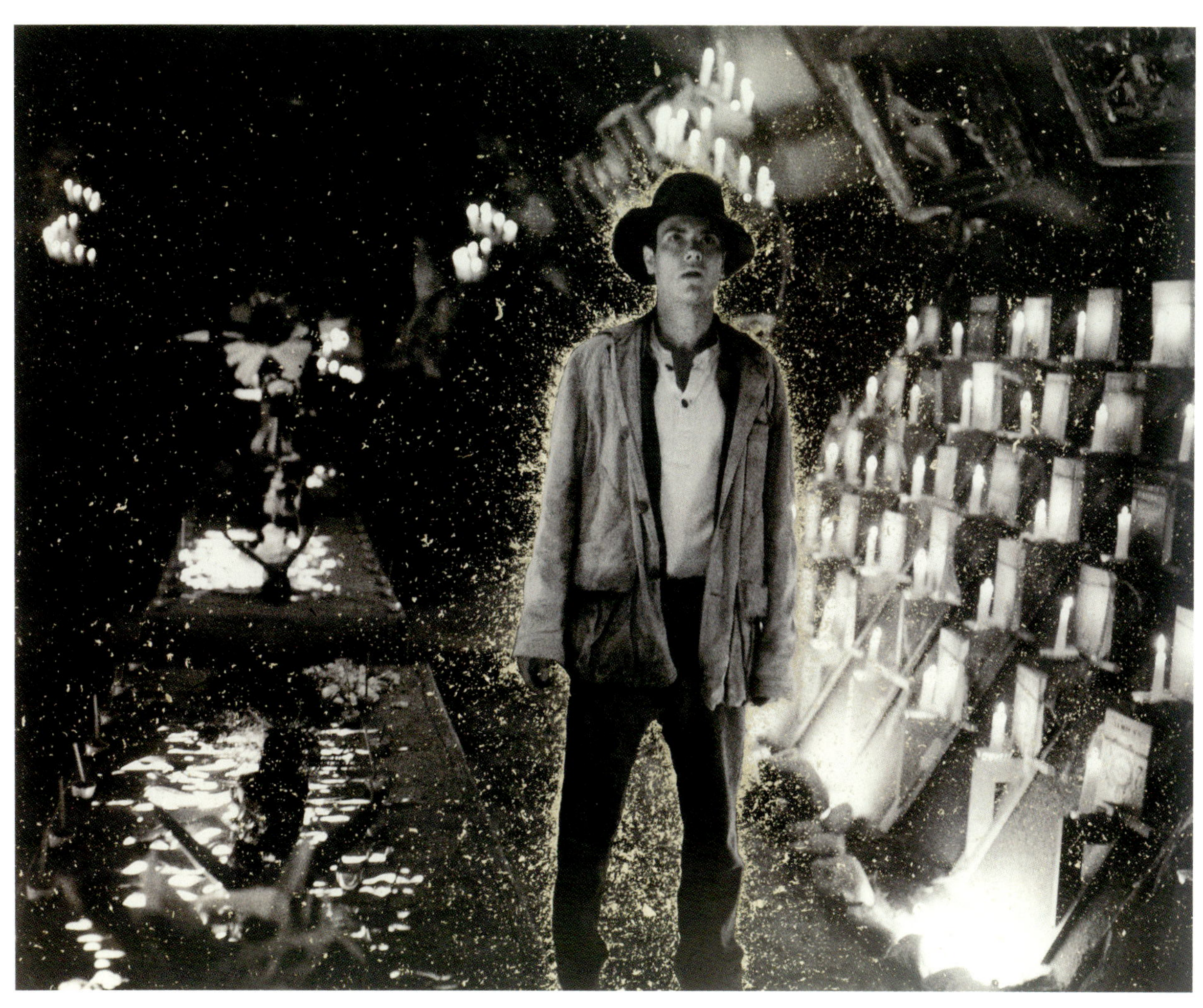

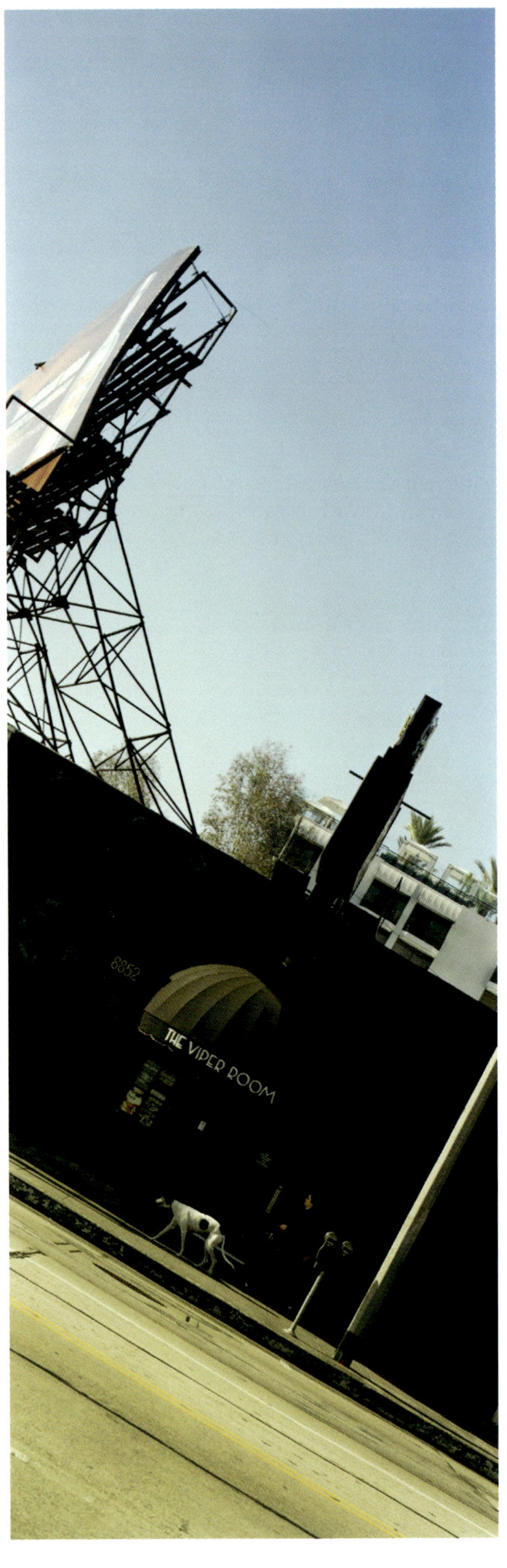
8852
THE VIPER ROOM

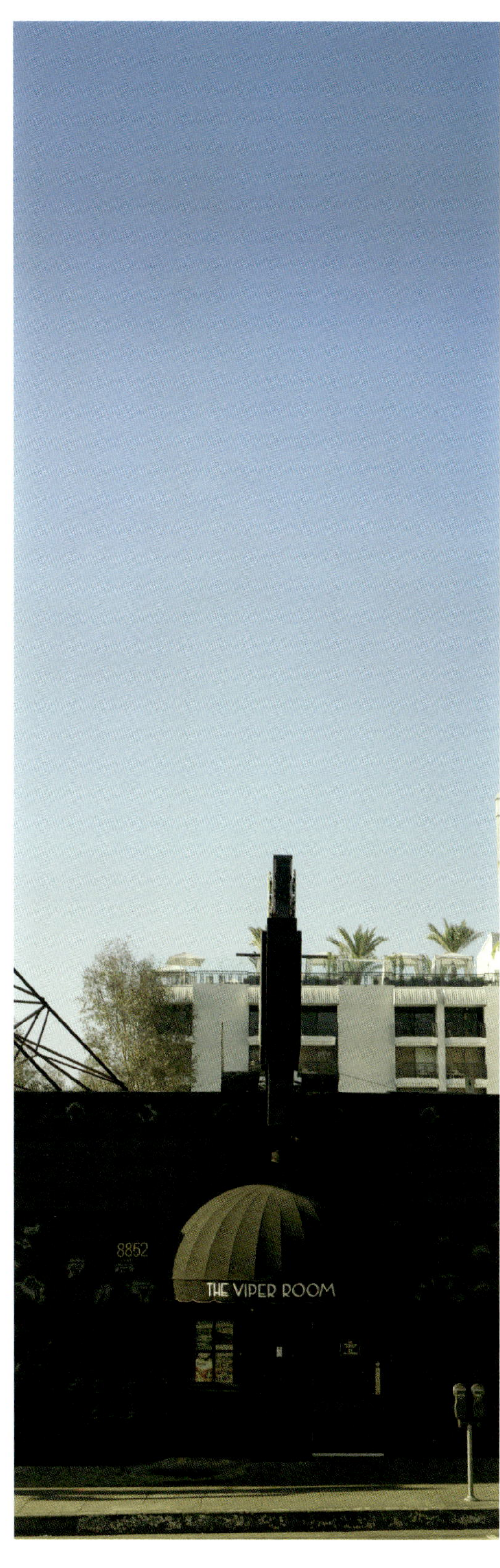
8852
THE VIPER ROOM

Exhibition Checklist

Shadow, 2010
High-definition video, color, five-channel surround sound
13:30 minutes
Edition of 5
Courtesy Team Gallery, New York; Max Wigram Gallery, London; Galería Helga de Alvear, Madrid; and Blum & Poe, Los Angeles

Dead Ringer, 2011
Three-channel high-definition video installation, three-channel sound
9:50 minutes
Edition of 5
Courtesy Team Gallery, New York; Max Wigram Gallery, London; Galería Helga de Alvear, Madrid; and Blum & Poe, Los Angeles

Shadow production still (Girl), 2010
C-print
72 x 110 inches
Edition of 5
Courtesy Team Gallery, New York

Shadow production still (Knife in the desert), 2010
C-print
80 x 64 inches
Edition of 5
Courtesy Team Gallery, New York

Shadow production still (Destroyed pink room), 2010
C-print
80 x 64 inches
Edition of 5
Courtesy Team Gallery, New York

Shadow production still (Dusk road), 2010
C-print
48 x 60 inches
Edition of 5
Courtesy Team Gallery, New York

Shadow production still (Girl in trailer), 2010
C-print
26 1/2 x 40 inches
Edition of 5
Courtesy Team Gallery, New York

The Viper Room (Easter), 2011
C-print
96 x 36 inches
Edition of 5
Courtesy Team Gallery, New York

Look Up and Stay in Touch (Cave), 1993/2011
Black-and-white Polaroid, gold marker
30 x 40 inches
Unique
Courtesy Team Gallery, New York

Look Up and Stay in Touch (Judy and River),
1993/2011
Black-and-white Polaroid, gold marker
30 x 40 inches
Unique
Courtesy Team Gallery, New York

Look Up and Stay in Touch (Deathbed),
1993/2011
Black-and-white Polaroid, gold marker
30 x 40 inches
Unique
Courtesy Team Gallery, New York

Look Up and Stay in Touch (Cave), 1993/2011
Black-and-white Polaroid, crushed moon
gold leaf
30 x 40 inches
Unique
Courtesy Team Gallery, New York

Look Up and Stay in Touch (Judy and River),
1993/2011
Black-and-white Polaroid, crushed moon
gold leaf
30 x 40 inches
Unique
Courtesy Team Gallery, New York

Look Up and Stay in Touch (Deathbed),
1993/2011
Black-and-white Polaroid, crushed moon
gold leaf
30 x 40 inches
Unique
Courtesy Team Gallery, New York

All works by
Slater Bradley and Ed Lachman

Slater Bradley

Born in 1975 in San Francisco. Lives and works in New York.

Education

1998 BA, University of California, Los Angeles, CA

Selected Solo Exhibitions

2011　*NEVER BET AGAINST ME*, Max Wigram Gallery, London
Slater Bradley and Ed Lachman: Shadow, Galería Helga de Alvear, Madrid
2010　*Slater Bradley and Ed Lachman: Shadow*, Whitney Museum of American Art, New York
CLEAN SLATE, PSM Galerie, Berlin
2009　*if we were immortal*, Team Gallery, New York; *Boulevard of broken dreams*, Max Wigram Gallery, London
Nothing changes how it used to be, De Hallen Haarlem, Haarlem, Netherlands
2008　*Perfect Empathy*, Taka Ishii Gallery, Tokyo
2007　*Hope from a Dark Place*, Blum & Poe, Los Angeles
The Unreleased Factory, Max Wigram Gallery, London
Tonic-Clonic, Galería Helga de Alvear, Madrid; Contemporary Art Museum, St. Louis
2006　*The Abandonments*, Team Gallery, New York
In a Mixed State, Max Wigram Gallery, London
2005　*Uncharted Settlements*, Taka Ishii Gallery, Tokyo
Intermission, Galerie Lisa Ruyter, Vienna
Lifetime Achievement Award, Savannah College of Art and Design, Savannah, GA (cat.)

Slater Bradley/MATRIX 216: The Year of the Doppelganger, Berkeley Art Museum and Pacific Film Archive, Berkeley, CA
Recent Acquisitions: Slater Bradley's Doppelganger Trilogy, Guggenheim Museum, New York
2004　*The Doppelganger Trilogy*, Blum & Poe, Los Angeles
STONED & DETHRONED, Team Gallery, New York
2003　*Nobody Gives a Fuck What You Go Do With Your Life*, MW Projects, London
Theory and Observation: New Work by Slater Bradley, Center for Curatorial Studies Museum, Bard College, Annandale-on-Hudson, NY (cat.)
2002　*Here are the Young Men*, Team Gallery, New York; Universitätsstadt Kaiserslautern, Kaiserslautern, Germany; Art + Public, Geneva
Keys in the Mailbox, Arndt & Partner, Berlin
2001　*Statements*, Art | 32 | Basel, Switzerland (under the auspices of Team Gallery)
Trompe Le Monde, Galerie Yvon Lambert, Paris
Home Town Hero, Refusalon, San Francisco
2000　*Special Projects Series*, P.S.1, Long Island City, NY
Charlatan, Team Gallery, New York
I was rooting for you, Irvine Fine Arts Center, Irvine, CA
1999　*The Fried Liver Attack*, Team Gallery, New York

Selected Group Exhibitions

2011　*Commercial Break*, Garage Projects, 54th Venice Biennale, Venice
The Last First Decade, Ellipse Foundation, Cascais, Portugal
Second Lives: Jeux masqués et autres Je, Casino Luxembourg, Luxembourg

2010   *Haunted*, Guggenheim Museum,
New York (cat.)
Kurt, Seattle Art Museum, Seattle
Sur le Dandysme, Centro Galego de
Arte Contemporanea,
Santiago de Compostella, Spain
Dracula Effect, Museo Universitario del
Chopo, Mexico City
HOW TO KILL A CELEBRITY,
Solyanka State Gallery, Moscow
The secret (still) knows, LAND,
Los Angeles

2009   *Incarnational Aesthetics*, NYCAMS,
New York
100 Years (version 2, ps1, nov 2009), P.S.1,
Long Island City, NY

2008   *The Ghost in the Machine*, Kunstnernes
Hus, Oslo
Still, Center for Visual Art,
Metropolitan State University, Denver
VOLUME(S), Casino Luxembourg,
Luxembourg
Rock My Religion, Domus Artium 02,
Salamanca, Spain
Young at Heart (Remix), Centro
Cultural de Cascais, Cascais, Portugal
Auto Stop, Malmö Konsthall, Malmö,
Sweden

2007   *The Present Order is the Disorder of the
Future*, Frans Hals Museum,
Haarlem, Netherlands
Stop, Look and Listen, Herbert F.
Johnson Museum of Art, Cornell
University, Ithaca, NY (traveled to
Haggerty Museum of Art, Marquette
University, Milwaukee)
*Sympathy for the Devil: Art and Rock
and Roll since 1967*, Museum of
Contemporary Art, Chicago (traveled
to the Museum of Contemporary
Art, Miami, and Musée d'Art
Contemporain, Montréal) (cat.)

2006   *Busan Biennale*, Busan Museum of
Modern Art, Busan, Korea (cat.)
Belief and Doubt, Aspen Art Museum,
Aspen, CO (cat.)

People, Madre Modern Art Museum,
Naples, Italy
Full House, Kunsthalle Mannheim,
Mannheim, Germany
Figures de l'Acteur, The Actor's Paradox,
Collection Lambert, Avignon, France
Youth of Today, Schirn Kunsthalle,
Frankfurt

2005   *The Gravity in Art*, De Appel
Foundation, Amsterdam
Superstars: The Principle of Reknown,
Kunsthalle Wien, Vienna (traveled
to Kunsthallen Brandts, Odense,
Denmark, DA2: Domus Artium 2002,
Salamanca, Spain)
*STAR STAR: Toward the Center of
Attention*, Contemporary Arts Center,
Cincinnati
Video-Musica-Video, Museo Reina
Sofia, Madrid

2004   *I Feel Mysterious Today*, Institute of
Contemporary Art,
Palm Beach, FL (cat.)
A Very Liquid Heaven, The Tang
Museum, Saratoga Springs, NY (cat.)
*Will Boys Be Boys?: Questioning
Adolescent Masculinity in Contemporary
Art*, The Salina Art Center, Salina,
KS (traveled to Museum of
Contemporary Art, Denver; The
Herbert F. Johnson Museum of
Art, Cornell University, Ithaca, NY;
Gulf Coast Museum of Art, Largo,
FL; Indianapolis Museum of Art,
Indianapolis) (cat.)
Stalemate, Museum of
Contemporary Art, Chicago
The Yugoslav Biennial, Vrsac, Serbia (cat.)
Whitney Biennial, Whitney Museum of
American Art, New York (cat.)
Playlist, Palais de Tokyo, Paris (cat.)

2003   *When Darkness Falls*, Gallery 400,
University of Illinois, Chicago
(traveled to Midway Contemporary
Art, Saint Paul, MN)

An Enquiry into those Kinds of Distress which excite agreeable Sensations (1773): Slater Bradley and Banks Violette, Team Gallery, New York
Someone to Watch Over Me, SMART Project Space, Amsterdam

2002   *Music/Video,* Musée d'Art Moderne et Contemporain, Strasbourg, France
Dark Spring, Ursula Blickle Stiftung, Kraichtal, Germany (cat.)

2001   *Casino 2001,* Stedelijk Museum voor Actuele Kunst, Ghent, Belgium (cat.)
Metropolis Now, Borusan Centre for Culture and Arts, Istanbul, Turkey (traveled to Museo Reina Sofia, Madrid, Spain)
Schau mir in die Augen, Kleines!, Kunsthalle Fridericianum, Kassel, Germany (cat.)
In a Lonely Place, National Museum of Photography, Film, and Television, Bradford, UK

Selected Bibliography

2011   Oliver Basciano, "Eternal Adolescence," *ArtReview,* January/February, 84–89.

2010   Andrew Hultkrans, "Dead Again," *Artforum.com,* November 2.
Mark Rappolt, "We Care A Lot," *ArtReview,* October, 72–74.
Micah Malone, "Kurt," *Artforum.com,* July 1.
Marina Cashan, "Live Souls," *Modern Painters,* March, 32–34.

2009   Elisabeth Kley, "Slater Bradley: Immortal Beloved," *Artnet.com,* December.
Martin Coomer, "Slater Bradley: Boulevard of Broken Dreams," *Art Review.com,* September.
Elisabeth Kley, "Slater Bradley: Perfect Empathy," *Eyemazing Magazine,* Spring, 6–16.

2008   Carrie Paterson, "Slater Bradley: Blum & Poe," *Flash Art,* January/February, 148–149.

2007   Tyler Coburn, "Slater Bradley: Man in the Mirror," *ArtReview,* December, 10, 74–77.
Brian Sholis, "Slater Bradley," *Artforum,* February, 295.

2006   Benjamin Genocchio, "Slater Bradley," *The New York Times,* December 8, E29.
Elisabeth Kley, "Slater Bradley," *Time Out New York,* November 30, 76.
Daniel Kunitz, "Cinephile: Slater Bradley," *ArtReview,* November, 46.
Pelin Uran, "Slater Bradley: An Interview," *UOVO* 11, 156–69.
Elisabeth Kley, "Critic's Pick: Slater Bradley," *ARTnews,* June, 168.
Martin Herbert, "Slater Bradley," *Time Out London,* May 3–10, 41.
Charlotte Bonham-Carter, "Showdown," *ArtReview,* March, 25.
Melissa E. Feldman, "Slater Bradley at Berkeley Art Museum and Blum & Poe" *Art in America,* January, 128–129.

2005   Melissa Lo, "Slater Bradley," *Flash Art,* March–April, 117–18.
Kley, Elisabeth, "The Disappearing Subject: Looking for Slater Bradley," *PAJ: A Journal of Performance and Art,* vol. 27, no. 1 (January): 102–107.
Slater Bradley, "Speak Memory: Reflections on the Doppelganger Trilogy," *PAJ: A Journal of Performance and Art,* vol. 27, no. 1 (January): 108–10.

2004   Lucas Hildebrand, "Grainy Days and Mondays: *Superstar* and Bootleg Aesthetics," *Camera Obscura 57,* vol. 19, no. 3 (December): 56–91.
Holly Willis, "The Doppelganger Trilogy," *LA Weekly,* December 24–30, 74.
Kyoko Wada, "Boys' Life: Slater Bradley," *Brutus,* August, 90–93, 116.

Michael Wilson, "I, Assassin,"
Frieze, May, 107.
Elizabeth Schambelan, "Slater
Bradley," *Artforum.com,* February 23.
Salden, Mark, "Buried Treasures," *Art
Review,* January, 37–38.

2003 Clay Weiner, "The Importance of
Being Slater Bradley," *Dazed and
Confused,* November, 100–104.
Simon Watson, "Post Bubble," *Issue,*
Fall, 118–39.
Jane Harris, "An Enquiry into those
Kinds of Distress which excite
agreeable Sensations (1773)," *Time
Out New York,* October 2, 63.
Benjamin Genocchio, "Video and
Photographs That Teeter on the Edge,"
The New York Times, August 17, 7.
Cohen, Michael, "Slater Bradley at
Team," *Flash Art International,* July/
September, 118.
Cotter, Holland, "Art in Review:
Slater Bradley," *The New York Times,*
May 17, E35.
Schwendener, Martha, "Slater Bradley,"
Time Out New York, May 23–30, 76.

2001 Charles-Arthur Boyer, "Jonathan
Horowitz and Slater Bradley, Galerie
Yvon Lambert," *Art Press,* June, 79–80.
Elizabeth Kley, "In Search of False
Time: Slater Bradley/T.J. Wilcox/Isaac
Julien," *PAJ: A Journal of Performance
and Art,* no. 68 (May): 61–67.
Max Henry, "Slater Bradley at Team,"
Art in America, April, 144.
David Hunt, "Slater Bradley," *Frieze,*
March, 98.

2000 Margaret Sundell, "Slater Bradley,"
Artforum, November, 157.
Jeremy Lin, "Prodigies: View Master,"
Surface, no. 26 (November): 1, 108, 110.
Robert Mahoney, "Slater Bradley," *Time
Out New York,* September 21–28, 69.
Roberta Smith, "Art in Review:
Slater Bradley," *The New York Times*,
September 15, E33.

Public Collections

Berkeley Art Museum and Pacific Film
Archive, University of California, Berkeley, CA
Center for Curatorial Studies Museum, Bard
College, Annandale-on-Hudson, NY
David Roberts Art Foundation, London
The Ellipse Foundation, Cascais, Portugal
Frans Hals Museum | De Hallen Haarlem,
Haarlem, Netherlands
Fundación Helga de Alvear, Cáceres, Spain
Hamburger Kunsthalle, Hamburg
Herbert F. Johnson Museum, Cornell
University, Ithaca, NY
Jumex Collection, Mexico City
The Kramlich Collection, San Francisco
Los Angeles County Museum of Art,
Los Angeles
Museum of Contemporary Art, Los Angeles
The Museum of Modern Art, New York
New Orleans Museum of Art, New Orleans
Progressive Collection, Cleveland
The Solomon R. Guggenheim Museum,
New York
21C Museum, Louisville, KY
U.B.S. Collection, Zurich
Whitney Museum of American Art, New York
Zabludowicz Collection, London

Ed Lachman

Born in 1946 in Morristown, NJ.
Lives and works in New York.

Education

1965 BA, Harvard University,
Cambridge, MA
1966–8 University of Tours, France
1969 BFA, Ohio University, Athens, OH

Filmography

Cinematographer

Paradies (2011; Ulrich Seidl) - *Mildred Pierce* (2011; Todd Haynes) - *Howl* (2010; Rob Epstein, Jeffrey Friedman) - *Collapse* (2009; Chris Smith) - *Life During Wartime* (2009; Todd Solondz) - *I'm Not There* (2007; Todd Haynes) - *Import/Export* (2007; Ulrich Seidl) - *Hounddog* (2007; Deborah Kampmeier) - *The Music of Regret* (2006; Laurie Simmons) - *A Prairie Home Companion* (2006; Robert Altman) - *Stryker* (2004; Noam Gonick) – *Moonlight Mile* (2002; Brad Silberling) - *Far from Heaven* (2002; Todd Haynes) - *Ken Park* (2002; Larry Clark, Ed Lachman) - *S1m0ne* (2002; Andrew Niccol) - *Erin Brockovich* (2000; Steven Soderbergh) - *The Virgin Suicides* (1999; Sofia Coppola) - *The Limey* (1999; Steven Soderbergh) - *Why Do Fools Fall in Love* (1998; Gregory Nava) - *Selena* (1997; Gregory Nava) - *Touch* (1997; Paul Schrader) - *My Family* (1995; Gregory Nava) - *Theremin: An Electronic Odyssey* (1995; Steven M Martin) - *Dark Blood* (1993; George Sluizer) - *My New Gun* (1992; Stacy Cochran) - *Light Sleeper* (1992; Paul Schrader) - *London Kills Me* (1991; Hanif Kureishi) - *Mississippi Masala* (1991; Mira Nair) - *Soldiers of Music* (1991; Bob Eisenhardt) - *Backtrack* (1990; Dennis Hopper billed as Alan Smithee) - *The Local Stigmatic* (1990; David F Wheeler) - *Less Than Zero* (1987; Marek Kanievska) - *Chuck Berry Hail! Hail! Rock 'n' Roll* (1987; Taylor Hackford) - *Making Mr. Right* (1987; Susan Seidelman) - *True Stories* (1986; David Byrne) - *Mother Theresa* (1986; Ann Petrie) - *Stripper* (1986; Jerome Gary) - *El día que me quieras* (1986; Sergio Dow) - *Ornette: Made in America* (1985; Shirley Clarke) - *Tokyo-Ga* (1985; Wim Wenders) - *Desperately Seeking Susan* (1985; Susan Seidelman) - *R.A.B.L.* (1985; Patrice M. Regnier) - The Look (1985; Robert Guralnick) - *In Our Hands* (1984; Robert Richter) - *Docu Drama* (1984; Ronee Blakley) - *Les Petites Guerres* (1982; Maroun Bagdadi) - *Say Amen, Somebody* (1982; George T. Nierenberg) - *They All Laughed* (1981; Peter Bogdanovich) - *Blank Generation* (1980; Ulli Lommel) - *Lightning over Water* (1980; Nick Ray, Wim Wenders) - *Union City* (1980; Mark Reichert) - *La Soufrière - Warten auf eine unausweichliche Katastrophe* (1977; Werner Herzog) - A Face (1977; John Grissmer) - *The Lords of Flatbush* (1974; Martin Davidson & Steve Verona)

Director

Hearts of Africa (2010) - *Life for a Child* (2008) - *Cell Stories* (2004) - *Ken Park (*2002, with Larry Clark) − *Lou Reed/John Cale: Songs for Drella, an Homage to Andy Warhol* (1990) - *Imagining America* (Episode : "Get Your Kicks on Route 66") - *The Last Trip to Harrisburg/ The Blue Train* (1984) - *Report from Hollywood* (1982) - *A Family Affair* (1979)

Awards

Camerimage: (for body of work) Cinematographer - Director Duo Award (with Todd Haynes) Gold Frog

Mildred Pierce: Nomination for Best Cinematography in a Television Miniseries - Emmy Awards, Cinematographer

I'm Not There: Bronze Frog - Camerimage

Far from Heaven: Outstanding Visual Contribution for Cinematography – Venice Film Festival, Academy Awards Nomination for Best Cinematography 2003, American Society of Cinematographers Award for Outstanding Achievements in Cinema and Photography, Silver Frog – Camerimage, Independent Spirit Award, Cholotrudis Award, Los Angeles Film Critics Award for Best Cinematography, New York Film Critics Association Award for Best Cinematography, Chicago Film Critics Association Award for Best Cinematography, Seattle Film Critics Award for Best Cinematography, Dallas Film Critics Award for Best Cinematography, Phoenix Film Critics Award for Best Cinematography, Florida Film Critics Award for Best Cinematography, Satellite Award for Best Cinematography, National Film Critics Society Award for Best Cinematography.

Ken Park: Golden Spike Nomination for Best Film – Valladolid International Film Festival (with Larry Clark)

The Virgin Suicides: Sierra Award for Best Cinematography – Las Vegas Film Critics Society Awards

Light Sleeper: Best Cinematography – Independent Spirit Awards

True Stories: Nomination for Best Cinematography – Independent Spirit Awards

El día que me quieras (The Day You Love Me): Golden Precolumbian Circle Award for Best Cinematography – Bogata Film Festival

Selected Exhibitions and Festival Screenings

2011
Slater Bradley and Ed Lachman: Shadow, Galería Helga de Alvear, Madrid, Spain
A Tribute to Edward Lachman, Prague International Film Festival, Prague

2010
About Jenny Holzer, DOKU ARTS International Festival on Films on Art, Berlin (with Claudia Müller)
Slater Bradley and Ed Lachman: Shadow, Whitney Museum of American Art, New York

2009
Ed Lachman Retrospective, KunstFilmBiennale, Cologne
Museum Ludwig, Cologne

2008
Exposure Checks: Polaroids and Images by Ed Lachman, Brooklyn Academy of Music, New York
The Cinematography of Ed Lachman, BAM Cinématek, New York

2006
The Music of Regret (directed by Laurie Simmons; cinematography by Ed Lachman), The Museum of Modern Art, New York, and Tate Modern, London

2005
Jeonju International Film Festival South Korea (Tribute and Masterclass)
"Cell Stories," *Documentary Fortnight*, The Museum of Modern Art, New York

2002
A Tribute to Ed Lachman, Vienna International Film Festival

Book Projects

Chausse-Trappes, Paris: Editions de Minuit, 1981, with contributions by Elieba Levine and Alain Robbe-Grillet

Acknowledgments
Heidi Zuckerman Jacobson

It is a great honor for the Aspen Art Museum to present *Slater Bradley and Ed Lachman: Look Up and Stay in Touch*, the final body of work in artist Slater Bradley's long-term doppelganger project. Museum exhibitions are always the result of the efforts of many individuals, and I am grateful to everyone who has helped realize this exhibition and publication.

I wish to thank my colleagues at the Aspen Art Museum: Development Assistant John Barker, Visitor Services Assistant Leslie Bixel, Executive Assistant to the Director Sherry Black, Curatorial Assistant Kelly Carver, Development Coordinator Ellie Closuit, Youth Programs Manager Genna Collins, Chief Preparator and Facilities Manager Jonathan Hagman, Education Outreach Coordinator Annie Henninger, Special Events Director Jason L. Hurley, Finance and Administrative Director Karen Johnsen, Community Liaison Nicole Kinsler, Accounting Clerk Sallie Klein, Communications Director Jeff Murcko, Campaign Coordinator Grace Nims, Project Manager Mike O'Connor, Curator Jacob Proctor, Visitor Services Assistant Liza Rueckert, Deputy Director John-Paul Schaefer, Visitor Services Assistant Jennifer Schneider, Editor and Publications Manager Ryan Shafer, Education Curator Danielle Stephens, Adjunct Curator Matthew Thompson (Associate Curator for most of the time that this exhibition and catalogue were in preparation), Staff Photographer Karl Wolfgang, and Registrar and Manager of Exhibitions Luis Yllanes. I am indebted to each and every one of you for your hard work and proud of all that we are able to collectively accomplish.

I am extremely grateful for the financial assistance of the Aspen Art Museum's National Council. One hundred percent of its contributions go to support our exhibitions, and this show is no exception. The public programs for the exhibition are presented as part of the Questrom Lecture Series.

For their longstanding support for Slater's work and for their assistance in organizing this show and book, I would like to thank José Freire, Miriam Katzeff, and Jessica Witkin at Team Gallery in New York; Tim Blum and Jeff Poe at Blum & Poe, Los Angeles; Max Wigram at Max Wigram Gallery, London; and Helga de Alvear at Galería Helga de Alvear, Madrid.

I would also like to thank Chrissie Iles, Anne & Joel Ehrenkranz Curator at the Whitney Museum of American Art, and Mark Rappolt, Editor of *ArtReview* magazine, for their thoughtful engagement with Slater's work in the new essays they have contributed to this publication, edited by Ryan Shafer and beautifully designed by John Weir in consultation with the legendary Peter Saville.

And finally, my heartfelt thanks go to Slater and Ed. I believe that our conversation included in this publication details the productive rapport that the two developed, and I am grateful to have been able to facilitate not only their published dialogue but also to exhibit the products of their dynamic collaboration.

Slater Bradley and Ed Lachman

We would like to thank the Aspen Art Museum, Helga de Alvear, Tim Blum, Amanda Chapin, Natalie Curtis, Kevin Cummins, John DeBlau, Michael "Dirk" Drury, Don Faller and Double Wide Media, José Freire, Joaquín García, Steve Hamilton, Chrissie Iles, Miriam Katzeff, Laura and Bella, Susie Mascotte, The Mascotte Family, Haans Nicholas Mott, Philippe Piguet, Jeff Poe, Mark Rappolt, Jan Roelfs, Jenn Ruff, Peter Saville, Ryan Shafer, Mark Weiler, John Weir, Max Wigram, Jessica Witkin, Luis Yllanes, and Heidi, of course.

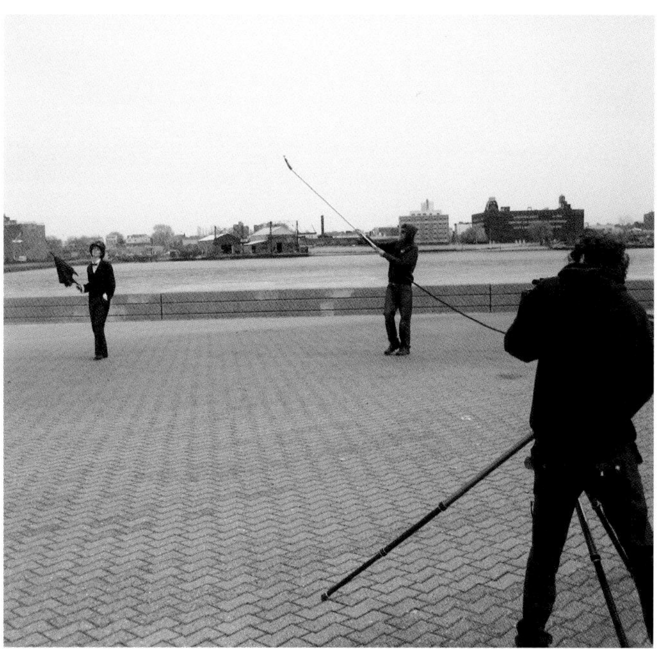

Look Up and Stay in Touch
is dedicated to Matty Mascotte.
Keep the rain coming.

Shadow / Dead Ringer

Slater Bradley and Ed Lachman

Doppelganger
Ben Brock

Young Girl
Elexess Bancroft

Line Producer / Double Wide Media
Don Faller

Editor Laura Israel	Colorist / Technicolor Tim Stippen
Assistant Editor Chelsea Smith	Assistant Camera / Set Photography Mark Weiler
Original Music Dale Stuckenbruck	Wardrobe / Props / Make-up Haans Nicholas Mott
Sound Design Steve Hamilton	Make-up Design Joelle Troisi
Sound Mixer / Dig It Audio Eric Gitelson	Talent & Location Coordinator Cheryl Leid

"Moon River"
Performed by Mika Bajinski
Performed Live at the Black Gardenia
London, July 2009

Produced by Team Gallery, New York
Max Wigram Gallery, London
Galería Helga de Alvear, Madrid
Blum & Poe Gallery, Los Angeles

Locations
Capitol Reef National Park, Hanksville,
Factory Butte, Utah
Luna Mesa Bar, Caineville, Utah

© Slater Bradley & Ed Lachman

<h1 align="center">Aspen Art Museum Staff</h1>

Heidi Zuckerman Jacobson
Chief Executive Officer and Director, Chief Curator

John Barker
Development Assistant

Leslie Bixel
Visitor Services Assistant

Sherry Black
Executive Assistant to the Director

Kelly Carver
Curatorial Assistant

Ellie Closuit
Development Coordinator

Genna Collins
Youth Programs Manager

Jonathan Hagman
Chief Preparator and Facilities Manager

Annie Henninger
Education Outreach Coordinator

Jason L. Hurley
Special Events Director

Karen Johnsen
Finance and Administrative Director

Nicole Kinsler
Community Liaison

Sallie Klein
Accounting Clerk

Jeff Murcko
Communications Director

Grace Nims
Campaign Coordinator

Mike O'Connor
Project Manager

Jacob Proctor
Curator

Liza Rueckert
Visitor Services Assistant

John-Paul Schaefer
Deputy Director

Jennifer Schneider
Visitor Services Assistant

Ryan Shafer
Editor and Publications Manager

Danielle Stephens
Education Curator

Matthew Thompson
Adjunct Curator

Karl Wolfgang
Staff Photographer

Luis Yllanes
Registrar and Manager of Exhibitions

Aspen Art Museum
Board of Trustees

John Phelan, *Co-President*
Paul Schorr, *Co-President*
Gayle Stoffel, *Secretary*
Jonathan Lee, *Treasurer*

Pam Alexander • Lance Armstrong • Charles Balbach • Jill Bernstein • Barbara Bluhm-Kaul • Charles Cunniffe • Theodor Dalenson • Domenico De Sole • Marcy Edelstein • Bruce Etkin • Marc Friedberg • Michael Gamson • Ramiro Garza • Robert Gersh • Carolyn Hamlet • Toby Devan Lewis • Debbie Lund • Laurie MacCaskill • Nancy Magoon • Nicola Marcus • Susan Marx • Judith Neisser • Alison Pincus • Carolyn Powers • Kelli Questrom • Mary Scanlan • Maria Smithburg • Simone Vickar

Aspen Art Museum
National Council

Eleanore and Domenico De Sole, *Chairs*
Pam Alexander, *Vice Chair*
Toby Devan Lewis, *Vice Chair*

Charles Balbach • Ms. Anne H. Bass • Maria and William Bell • Barbara and Bruce Berger • Marie and Robert Bergman • Jill and Jay Bernstein • Barbara and William Broeder • Melva Bucksbaum and Raymond Learsy • Nancy and Clint Carlson • Simona and Jerome Chazen • Rona and Jeffrey Citrin • Dathel and Tommy Coleman • Bunni and Paul Copaken • Isabella and Theodor Dalenson • Frances Dittmer • Holly and David Dreman • Stefan Edlis and Gael Neeson • Richard Edwards • Suzanne Farver • Christy Ferer • Marilyn and Larry Fields • Barbara and Michael Gamson • Gabriela and Ramiro Garza • Linda and Bob Gersh • Jan and Ronald Greenberg • Diane and Bruce Halle • Sharon and John Hoffman • Phyllis Hojel • Toni and Daniel Holtz • Ann and Edward Hudson • Holly Hunt • Fern Hurst • Soledad and Robert Hurst • Allison and Warren Kanders • Sylvia and Richard Kaufman • Barbara S. Bluhm-Kaul and Don Kaul • Erica and Jeff Keswin • Sally and Jonathan Kovler • Evelyn and Leonard Lauder • Barbara and Jonathan Lee • Vicki and Kent Logan • Karen and Courtney Lord • Marianne and Sheldon Lubar • Nancy and Robert Magoon • Marlene and Fred Malek • Nicola and Jeff Marcus • Susan and Larry Marx • Nancy and Peter Meinig • Meryl and Robert Meltzer • Gail and Alec Merriam • Lisa and Will Mesdag • Jane and Marc Nathanson • Judith Neisser • Erin and Paul Pariser • John and Amy Phelan • Carolyn and William Powers • Allen and Kelli Questrom • Katie and Amnon Rodan • Jeanne Greenberg-Rohatyn and Nicolas Rohatyn • Michelle and Jason Rubell • Lisa and John Runyon • Cari and Michael Sacks • Pamela and Arthur Sanders • Mary and Patrick Scanlan • Danner and Arno Schefler • Barbara and Eugene Schmitt • Debra and Dennis Scholl • June and Paul Schorr • Vicki and Ronald Simms • Shirley and Albert Small • Sue and Lester Smith • Sandy and Art Soares • Mary and David Solomon • Sara Dodd-Spickelmier and Keith Spickelmier • Jennifer and David Stockman • Gayle and Paul Stoffel • Ellen and Steve Susman • Melissa and Russell Wight • Mary and Harold Zlot

List of Illustrations

pp. 38–39: Slater Bradley and Ed Lachman, *Shadow* production still (Girl in trailer), 2010. C-print. 26 1/2 x 40 inches. Edition of 5. Courtesy Team Gallery, New York.

p. 41: Slater Bradley and Ed Lachman, *Shadow* production still (Destroyed pink room), 2010. C-print. 80 x 64 inches. Edition of 5. Courtesy Team Gallery, New York.

p. 43: Christopher Lloyd as Dr. Emmett Brown (center) in *Back to the Future* (Robert Zemeckis, 1985). Courtesy NBCUniversal Archives and Collections.

p. 44: Vladimir Nabokov. Courtesy CorbisImages.com.

p. 45: Slater Bradley, *Dark Night of the Soul*, 2005/06. Digital video, sound. 8:05 minutes. Dimensions variable. Edition of 3. Courtesy of Team Gallery.

p. 46 (left): Slater Bradley, *Factory Ikon*, 2000/04. C-print. 80 x 64 inches. Edition of 3. Courtesy of Team Gallery.

p. 46 (center): Slater Bradley, *I hate myself and want to die*, 2003/04. C-print. 80 x 64 inches. Edition of 3. Courtesy of Team Gallery.

p. 46 (right): Slater Bradley, *The Animals (outtake)*, 2004. Silver gelatin print. 24 x 16 inches. Edition of 9. Courtesy of Team Gallery.

p. 47: Slater Bradley, *Marijuana*, 2004. Magazines, custom frame. 30 x 40 inches. Collection of Mark Grotjahn.

pp. 52–71: Slater Bradley and Ed Lachman, *Shadow*, 2010. High-definition video, color, five-channel surround sound. 13:30 minutes. Edition of 5. Courtesy Team Gallery, New York; Max Wigram Gallery, London; Galería

Helga de Alvear, Madrid; and Blum & Poe, Los Angeles.

pp. 78–79: Ed Lachman, exposure test black-and-white Polaroids taken on the set of *Dark Blood* (George Sluizer, 1993).

p. 89: Slater Bradley, *Lachman's Legacy*, 2009. Oil on linen, Japanese red leaf and moon gold leaf. 24 x 24 inches. Collection of the artist.

pp. 90–95: Slater Bradley and Ed Lachman, *Dead Ringer*, 2011. Three-channel high-definition video installation, three-channel sound. 9:50 minutes. Edition of 5. Courtesy Team Gallery, New York; Max Wigram Gallery, London; Galería Helga de Alvear, Madrid; and Blum & Poe, Los Angeles.

p. 97: Slater Bradley and Ed Lachman, *Look Up and Stay in Touch (Deathbed)*, 1993/2011. Black-and-white Polaroid, crushed moon gold leaf. 30 x 40 inches. Unique. Courtesy Team Gallery, New York.

p. 99: Slater Bradley and Ed Lachman, *Look Up and Stay in Touch (Judy and River)*, 1993/2011. Black-and-white Polaroid, crushed moon gold leaf. 30 x 40 inches. Unique. Courtesy Team Gallery, New York.

p. 101: Slater Bradley and Ed Lachman, *Look Up and Stay in Touch (Cave)*, 1993/2011. Black-and-white Polaroid, crushed moon gold leaf. 30 x 40 inches. Unique. Courtesy Team Gallery, New York.

p. 102: Slater Bradley and Ed Lachman, *The Viper Room (Good Friday)*, 2011. Courtesy of the artists.

p. 103: Slater Bradley and Ed Lachman, *The Viper Room (Easter)*, 2011. C-print. 96 x 36 inches. Edition of 5. Courtesy Team Gallery, New York.

This publication accompanies the exhibition Slater Bradley and Ed Lachman: *Look Up and Stay in Touch*, organized by the Aspen Art Museum.

Aspen Art Museum
December 9, 2011–February 5, 2012

Published by Aspen Art Press

aspenartmuseum

590 North Mill Street, Aspen, CO, 81611
United States
aspenartmuseum.org

Copyright © 2011 Aspen Art Museum, the artists, and the authors. All rights reserved. No part of this book may be reproduced in any manner without the written consent of the publishers.

A CIP record for this book is available from the Library of Congress
ISBN 978-0-934324-53-3
Edited by Ryan Shafer
Catalogue design by John Weir in consultation with Peter Saville
Printed by Perry/Granger & Associates, San Francisco, CA
Printed and bound in Belmont, CA

Available through Artbook, LLC and D.A.P. | Distributed Art Publishers
155 Sixth Avenue, 2nd Floor, New York, N.Y., 10013
Tel: (212) 627-1999
Fax: (212) 627-9484

This exhibition is funded in part by the AAM National Council. General exhibition support is provided by The Andy Warhol Foundation for the Visual Arts. Exhibition lectures are presented as part of the Questrom Lecture Series.